TEARS *of* JOY

for

Mothers

TEARS *of* JOY
for

Mothers

*A Collection of Stories for
Your Heart and Soul*

Compiled and Edited by

JOE WHEELER

W PUBLISHING GROUP
A Division of Thomas Nelson Publishers
Since 1798
www.wpublishinggroup.com

Tears of Joy for Mothers
© 2006 Joseph L. Wheeler.

Published by W Publishing Group, a Division of Thomas Nelson, Inc., P.O. Box 141000, Nashville, TN 37214.

W Publishing Group books may be purchased in bulk for educational, business, fundraising, or sales promotional use. For information, please email SpecialMarkets@ThomasNelson.com.

Published in association with WordServe Literary Group, 10152 Knoll Circle, Highlands Ranch, CO 80130.

Visit the author at www.joewheelerbooks.com.

Cover Design: Josh Huhn, Design Point Inc.
Interior Design: Lori Lynch, Book and Graphic Design, Nashville, TN
Illustrations: From the library of Joe Wheeler

Library of Congress Cataloging-in-Publication Data

Tears of joy for mothers : a collection of stories for your heart and soul / compiled and edited by Joe Wheeler.
    p. cm.
  Summary: "Collection of stories, old and new, for and about mothers"— Provided by publisher.
  ISBN 0-8499-1190-7 (tradepaper)
  1. Mothers—Fiction. 2. Motherhood—Fiction. 3. Short stories, American. I. Wheeler, Joe L., 1936–
PS648.M59T43 2006
813'.010835252—dc22   2005037900

Printed in the United States of America
06 07 08 09 10 RRD 9 8 7 6 5 4 3 2 1

It is fitting that I honor the remarkable woman
described in my Introduction, "My Mother's Scrapbooks,"
with one last posthumous tribute.

I hereby dedicate this collection of mother-related
stories to my beloved mother,
BARBARA LEININGER WHEELER
(1912–2005)

CONTENTS

ACKNOWLEDGMENTS

"My Mother's Scrapbooks," by Joseph Leininger Wheeler. Copyright © 2005. Printed by permission of the author.

"The Day Mother Cried," by Gerald Moore. Published in December 1980 *Reader's Digest*. Reprinted by permission of the author and Reader's Digest, Inc.

"The Littlest Orphan and the Christ Baby," by Margaret E. Sangster Jr. Included in Sangster's anthology, *The Littlest Orphan and Other Christmas Stories* (New York: Round Table Press, 1928). If anyone can provide knowledge of earliest publication source of this old story, please send to Joe Wheeler (P.O. Box 1246, Conifer, CO 80433).

"The Mustard Plaster," author unknown.

"The Song of Songs," by Mabel McKee. Published in *The Youth's Instructor*, April 28, 1931. Reprinted by permission of Joe L. Wheeler (P.O. Box 1246, Conifer, CO 80433) and Review and Herald Publishing, Hagerstown, Maryland.

"Third Time's the Charm," by Katherine Holland Brown. Published in *The Christian Herald*, December 15, 1923. Reprinted by permission of Christian Herald, Inc.

"Apple Blossoms," author unknown.

ACKNOWLEDGMENTS

"The Stepmother," by Margaret Weymouth Jackson. First published in *Cosmopolitan*. Copyright © 1948 by Margaret Weymouth Jackson. Reprinted by permission of Harold Ober Associates.

"Zachary's Angel," by Ruth Lees Olson. Published in *The Youth's Instructor*, July 10, 1934. Reprinted by permission of Joe L. Wheeler (P.O. Box 1246, Conifer, Co. 80433) and Review and Herald Publishing, Hagerstown, Maryland.

"When They All Came Home," by Agnes Sligh Turnbull. Included in Turnbull's anthology, *Old Home Town*, 1933. If anyone can provide knowledge of earliest publication source of this old story, please send to Joe Wheeler, P.O. Box 1246, Conifer, CO 80433.

"Story of Love," author unknown.

"Beautiful Dreamer," by Arthur Gordon. Included in Gordon's *A Touch of Wonder* (Old Tappan, N.J.: Fleming H. Revell, 1974). Reprinted by permission of Pamela Gordon.

"The Little Room," author unknown. Published in *Review and Herald*, June 28, 1934. Reprinted by permission of Joe L. Wheeler (P.O. Box 1246, Conifer, CO 80433) and Review and Herald Publishing, Hagerstown, Maryland.

"The New Neighbor," by Emma Gary Wallace. Published in *The Christian Herald*, March 5, 1927. Reprinted by permission of Christian Herald, Inc.

"Stella Solaris," by Joseph Leininger Wheeler. Copyright © 2005. Printed by permission of the author.

MY MOTHER'S SCRAPBOOKS

JOSEPH LEININGER WHEELER

Of all the legacies bequeathed to me by my mother, none do I value more than two well-traveled books of poetry. The covers are of wood, made by my father. And my mother illustrated the poems with pictures she clipped from magazines of long ago.

At the very heart of my mother's public performances were poems celebrating the laughter and tears of the home. Of what it means to be a mother or a father. Of a child's impact on a marriage. Of one of God's greatest gifts to mothers: a sense of humor. Of the tragic brevity of childhood and the fragility of life. Of romance with the boy/man and its central role in home security.

My brother, Romayne; sister, Marjorie; and I grew up listening to our mother read poems of romance. These poems, along with our parents' enduring courtship, created a solid foundation for our own marriages that no earthquake or storm could ever shake.

Here are some of the home-related poems my mother loved best—all of which came from her beloved scrapbooks.

Little Steenie

Why we so loved this poem, we didn't then know. Perhaps its charm had to do with Steenie's naughtiness, so like our own. Maybe we loved it because the words reassured us that no matter how awfully we behaved, our mother's love was a God-given constant.

Not surprisingly, this poem spoke to hearts everywhere, and rarely did my mother give a public poetry reading when somebody didn't request, "*Please*, won't you do 'Little Steenie'?"

Sturdy Steenie, rosy-cheeked, bright-eyed,
Standing at the open door,
Bidding me good-bye with kisses
And with promises a score—
"I'll be just as good as apples,
'Bey my aunties and not cry,
Not tease Mabe and wake the baby,
Kiss me, Mama,—and good-bye."

So I started, musing softly on the blessings God had given
In my children—"Surely," said I, "They are
Cherubs strayed from heaven;
Hearts so full of tender loving,
Eyes with earnest impulse bright—
Round them still there seems to linger
Halos of celestial light."

Two hours later, home returning,
Languidly, with weary feet,
Standing in the selfsame doorway,
Little Mabe, I chanced to greet.
Bright blue eyes all flushed with weeping,
Lips aquiver, cheeks aflame,
Eager to pour her sorrows
Into Mama's ear, she came.

"Mama, Steenie's been so naughty—
First, he told Aunt Sally, 'Won't!'
Then he scratched my little table
Though I begged him, please, to don't.
Then he screeched and waked the baby
Frightened him most to a fit,
And when Aunt Sally said he's naughty—
Said he didn't care a bit.

"Then he made a face at dolly,
Said she was an ugly sing,
Said someday he's goin' to tie her
To the doorknob with a string.
Then I told him, if he did it,
You would send him right to bed,
Then he thumped me on the shoulder,
See the place,—it's awful red.

"When he saw you comin', Mama,
He hid hisself behind the door,
And he's wearin' out his slippers

Poundin' with 'em on the floor.
Mama, if he is so very naughty,
Does so many drefful things,—
Will he ever be an angel
Up in heaven with shiny wings?"

With a sudden jerk, my visions
Of celestial cherubs fled,
Frowningly, my brows contracted,
And in accents stern, I said,—
"Come to me, you naughty fellow,
What are all these things I hear,
Rude to Auntie, striking sister,
I must punish you, I fear."

From his stronghold came the culprit,
Seeming not at all afraid,
Round his mouth the dimples lurking,
Brown eyes beaming, undismayed.
By my knee he took his station,
Small defiance in his air,
Answering only to my chidings
Saucily,—"I doesn't care."

In my eyes, the teardrops started,
Anger giving place to pain.
"Oh, my baby, how you grieve me,
Are my teachings all in vain?"
Suddenly, two arms went round me,
Little fingers softly drew

Down my quivering lips to meet his, saying,
"Kiss me, Mama,—I loves you."

That was all of his confession
All his plea for pardoning grace,
Yet, I knew that I had conquered
By the lovelight in his face,—
So I gave him absolution
Though I pondered sadly still
On this mingled human nature—
Half of good and half of ill.

Inwardly, I prayed for wisdom,
Safe my little band to guide,
Through the perils that beset them
Hedge them in on every side.
And an answer seemed to come,
Softly falling from above,
"Safest guard and guide, Oh, Mother,
Is the holy power of love."

                                    —*Author Unknown*

"Silver and Gold"

We loved this poem just as much as "Little Steenie," perhaps
because the rhythm of the lines captivated us, or maybe
because the poem's image of a cheerful mother working all day
without any expectation of reward was mirrored in our own
mother's life.

Looking back, I see that this poem, so often requested at
Mother's public readings, balanced the naughtiness of Steenie

with an example we children wished to follow, even before we
knew the meaning of the lovely sounding words.

> The little maid sat in the high-backed pew
>   And raised to the pulpit her eyes of blue,
> The prayers were long and the sermon was grand
>   But oh, it was hard to understand.
> But the beautiful text sank deep in her heart
>   Which the preacher made of his sermon a part.
> "Silver and gold have I none," said he,
>   "But such as I have give I to Thee."
> And the good old parson looked down and smiled
>   At the earnest gaze of the little child.
>
> The little maid carried home the word
>   Determined to use it as chance might afford.
> She saw her mother unceasingly
>   Toil for the needs of the family,
> So she cheerfully helped the whole day through
>   And did with her might what her hands found to do.
> "Silver and gold have I none," said she,
>   "But such as I have give I to thee."
> And the weary mother looked down and smiled
>   As she bent to kiss the little child.
>
> On her way to school at early morn,
>   She plucked the blooms by the wayside born,
> "For my teacher is often tired, I know,
>   For we're sometimes naughty, and we're
>   sometimes slow,

Perhaps these will help to lighten her task,"
 And she laid the flowers on the teacher's desk.
"Silver and gold have I none," said she,
 "But such as I have give I to thee."
And the happy teacher stopped and smiled
 As she joyfully thanked the little child.

As she played with her sister on the grass,
 She saw a dusty traveler pass,
"Poor soul," she said, "he is tired, I think,
 I will go and get him a nice cool drink."
So she hastened to get her little cup
 And dipped the sparkling nectar up,
"Silver and gold have I none," said she,
 "But such as I have give I to thee."
And the thirsty dusty traveler smiled
 As he took the cup from the little child.

Sweet and innocent, clad in white,
 She knelt by her little bed that night,
With a childish trust, she longed to bring
 Some gift to her Saviour and her King,
"So much from Thee, every day, I receive,
 But my heart is all that I have to give,
Silver and gold have I none," said she,
 "But such as I have give I to Thee."
And the Father above looked down and smiled
 As he took the great gift from the little child.
—Author Unknown

"I Give Him Half of Mine"

People have sometimes commented that our family seems so unselfish, since we don't keep track of how much a brother or sister receives. Only when I became an adult and saw homes torn by jealousy and greed did I realize how blessed we are. I attribute our family's collective unselfishness to Mother's consistent reading of this poem.

Ist a little orphan boy
at goes to school with me,
And he ain't got no ma or pa
cuz his folks is dead you see.
And when he sees my toys and things,
My, but his eyes *ist* shine.
And cuz he didn't have no toys,
I give him half of mine!

One day it's orful rainy
And he can't go back to where he works
for board and room to get his lunch,
and so I had some sandwiches and things
and he thought that was *ist* fine.
And cuz he didn't have no dinner,
I give him half of mine!

One day when I went down to fish,
he came along with me,
And when we're there,
he says he ist wished 'at he could fish.

You see, he's orful poor,
He brought a pole but didn't have a line;
And when I saw how bad he felt,
I give him half of mine!

One day I told my ma how he didn't have much fun,
He didn't have no ma or pa or aunt or anyone
And I told her that I thought that it would
be *ist* fine,—
That cuz he didn't have no ma or pa,
I'd give him half of mine.

He's not my brother really true,
He's ist an orphan, see.
So Ma said she'd take him cuz she knew he had no place to go.
I'm orful glad we got him
and Pa thinks it's *ist* fine
That since he didn't have no ma or pa
I'd give him half of mine!

"THE WORLD IS MINE"

Another poem Mother often recited had to do with attitude.
Since we were missionary children, with little of this world's
goods, we could have easily felt deprived. Easily, that is, if we
weren't hearing this poem so often!

Today upon a bus, I saw a lovely maid with golden hair;
I envied her—she seemed so gay—and wished I were as fair.
When suddenly she rose to leave, I saw her hobble down
the aisle;

She had one foot and wore a crutch, but as she passed,
　a smile.
　　　O God, forgive me when I whine;
　　　I have two feet—the world is mine!

And then I stopped to buy some sweets.
The lad who sold them had such charm.
I talked with him—he said to me,
"It's nice to talk with folks like you.
You see," he said, "I'm blind."
　　　O God, forgive me when I whine;
　　　I have two eyes—the world is mine!

Then walking down the street, I saw a child with eyes of blue.
He stood and watched the others play;
It seemed he knew not what to do.
I stopped a moment, then I said,
"Why don't you join the others, dear?"
He looked ahead without a word, and then
I knew, he could not hear.
　　　O God, forgive me when I whine;
　　　I have two ears—the world is mine!

With feet to take me where I'd go,
With eyes to see the sunset's glow,
With ears to hear what I would know,
　　　O God, forgive me when I whine;
　　　I'm blessed, indeed! The world is mine!
　　　　　　　　　　—*Author Unknown*

Mother knew by heart Longfellow's book-length poems *Evangeline* and *The Song of Hiawatha* from which come these lines she often recited:

As unto the bow the cord is,
So unto man is woman;
Though she bends him, she obeys him,
Though she draw him, yet she follows;
Useless each without the other!

"THE BRIDE"

Like so many of Mother's poems, the name of the author has long been separated from the poem itself. The oral tradition, of which Mother was a part, paid little attention to the source of a given work. It is because of this oral tradition that there are often irregularities in the scrapbook verse text, as Mother had to tinker with some of the rhymes to get them to work right. I belatedly discovered that very few of Mother's poems exist in books; they are her heritage from a vanished breed of folk poets and storytellers. What a tragic loss!

This one my mother often recited at weddings and bridal showers. As children, we were captivated by the poem. It is only now, so many years after first hearing it, that I realize that we were learning that life would be tough, with sorrow alternating with joy. It helped to prepare us for "until death do us part marriages."

Little lady at the altar,
Vowing by God's book and psalter,
To be faithful, fond, and true,
To the one who stands by you;
Think not that romance is ended,
And youth's curtain has descended,
And love's pretty play is done,—
It is only just begun!

Marriage, lovely little lady,
Is love's sunny path and shady,
Over which two hearts should wander
Of each other growing fonder,
As they tread to each to-morrow
With its joy and with its sorrow,
Bitter cares will someday find you,
Closer, closer, they will bind you,
If together you will bear them,
Cares grow sweet when lovers share them.
Love unites two happy mortals,
Brings them here to wedlock's portals,
And then blithely bids them go
Arm in arm through weal and woe.

Little lady, just remember,
Every year has its December,
Every rising sun, its setting,
Every life, its time of fretting,
And the honeymoon's sweet beauty,
Finds so soon the path of duty,

But keep faith when trouble tried,
And in joy you shall abide.

Little lady at the altar
Never let your courage falter.
Never stoop to unbelieving,
Even when your heart is grieving,
To what comes of wintry weather,
And disaster,—stand together,
Through life's fearful hours of night,
Love shall lead you to the light. . . .

"HOME"

Mother adored the poetry of Edgar A. Guest, the poet of the American home. She knew many of his poems by heart. This one, easily the most beloved poem Guest ever wrote, Mother used as a comparison piece to "The Bride." In it, we children were given an early reality check as to what raising a family would be like.

Mother never knew lasting homesteads during her life, for her minister-husband moved often. Yet we children instinctively knew that Guest was speaking in these lines not of wood and stones and glass, but of the fabric of hearts that are true to each other.

It takes a heap o' livin' in a house t' make it home,
A heap o' sun an' shadder, an' ye sometimes have t' roam
Afore ye really 'preciate the things ye lef' behind,
An' hunger fer 'em somehow, with 'em allus on yer mind.
It don't make any differunce how rich ye get t' be,

How much yer chairs an' tables cost, how great
    yer luxury;
It ain't home t' ye, though it be the palace of a king,
Until somehow yer soul is sort o' wrapped round
    everything.

Home ain't a place that gold can buy or get up
    in a minute;
Afore it's home there's got t' be a heap o' livin' in it;
Within the walls there's got t' be some babies
    born, and then
Right there ye've got t' bring 'em up t' women
    good, an' men;
And gradjerly, as time goes on, ye find ye wouldn't part
With anything they ever used—they've grown
    into yer heart:
The old highchairs, the playthings, too, the
    little shoes they wore
Ye hoard; an' if ye could ye'd keep the thumb-
    marks on the door.

Ye've got t' weep t' make it home, ye've got t' sit an' sigh
An' watch beside a loved one's bed, an' know
    that Death is nigh;
An' in the stillness o' the night t' see Death's angel come,
An' close the eyes o' her that smiled, an' leave
    her sweet voice dumb.
Fer these are scenes that grip the heart, an'
    when yer tears are dried,
Ye find the home is dearer than it was, an' sanctified;

An' tuggin' at ye always are the pleasant memories
O' her that was an' is no more—ye can't escape from these.
Ye've got t' sing an' dance fer years, ye've got t' romp an' play,
An' learn t' love the things ye have by usin' 'em each day;
Even the roses 'round the porch must blossom year by year
Afore they 'come a part o' ye, suggestin' someone dear
Who used t' love 'em long ago, an' trained 'em jes t' run
The way they do, so's they would get the early mornin' sun;
Ye've got t' love each brick an' stone from cellar up t' dome:
It takes a heap o' livin' in a house t' make it home.

"THE PATH TO HOME"

Another of Guest's poems that Mother inserted into her scrapbook of most beloved poems is "The Path to Home," from
which come these lines:

There is nothing so important as the mother's lullabies
Filled with peace and sweet contentment when the moon
    begins to rise,
Nothing real, except the beauty, and the smile upon her face
And the shouting of the children as they scamper round
    the place. . . .

Indeed, Mother's smile, as she recited poetry to us and told
us stories, was our first heaven.

"A LESSON"

Recognizing how brief a time she would have with her children
at home, Mother would often recite this poem, reminiscent of

"The Cat's Cradle," about the futility of trying to relive opportunities that are now lost forever.

> Have you seen anywhere, a tall little lad
> And a small winsome lass of four?
> It was only today, barefooted and brown
> That they played by my kitchen door.
> It was only a day, or maybe a year,
> It couldn't be twenty, I know;
> They were shouting for me to help in their game,
> But I was too busy to go.
> Too busy with sweeping and dusting to play,
> And now they have silently wandered away.
>
> If by chance you hear of this slim little lad
> And a small winsome lassie of four;
> I pray you to tell me—to find them again
> I would search the whole world o'er.
> For somewhere I'm sure they'll be playing a game,
> And should they be calling to me
> To come out and help; O tell them I beg
> That I'm coming as fast as can be.
> For there's never a house could hold me today
> Should I hear them call me to join in their play.

CHANGES OF PACE

If all of Mother's poems had been moral agendas, we would have developed an immunity to their messages. But she wisely interspersed the didactic poems with all kinds of poetic changes of pace. For example, on a moonlit night, she'd send chills up our spines by launching into Alfred Noyes's "The Highwayman."

> The wind was a torrent of darkness among the gusty trees,
> The moon was a ghostly galleon tossed upon cloudy seas,
> The road was a ribbon of moonlight over the purple moor,
> And the highwayman came riding—
> > Riding—riding—
> The Highwayman came riding, up to the old inn door. . . .

Or perhaps she would recite Frank Desprez's hot-blooded "Lasca":

> She was alive in every limb
> With feeling, to the fingertips;
> And when the sun is like a fire,
> And sky one shining, soft sapphire,
> One does not drink in little sips.

Perhaps she'd recite that great Civil War horse poem "Kentucky Belle," by Constance Fenimore Woolson, with lines such as these:

> As I ran back to the log house at once there came a
> > sound—
> The ring of hoofs, galloping hoofs, trembling over the
> > ground,
> Coming into the turnpike out from the White Woman
> > Glen—
> Morgan, Morgan the raider, and Morgan's terrible men.

Perhaps she'd describe for us the mother at wit's end in the anonymous poem "Mother's Lament":

Baby's in the sugar bowl,
Brother's in the sink,
Puppy's in the baby's bed,
—And I'm supposed to think!

Wonder what to have for lunch,
Hope it doesn't rain,
Breakfast dishes to be done,
Time to wash again.

Run along,—you little scamp,
Let me concentrate,
Take the doggie with you—
Stay inside the gate.

Brother's lost his hat again,
Baby's nose is dripping,
Shoes and stockings cast away—
Brother's pants are slipping.

Soon they'll all be in the mud
Or more unlikely places.
Yes, mother's place is in the home—
A home for mental cases.

Or perhaps it would be our all-time favorite nonsense poem, written by an unknown poet, called, "The Moo-Cow-Moo":

My pa held me up to the moo-cow-moo
So close I could almost touch:
An' I fed him a couple of times or two
An' I wasn't a fraid' cat much.
But, ef my Pa goes into the house,
An' ef my mama goes too,
I jest keep still like a little mouse
'Cause the moo-cow-moo might moo!

The moo-cow-moo has a tail like a rope,
An' it's raveled down where it grows;
An' it's just like feelin' a piece of soap
All over the moo-cow's nose.

The moo-cow-moo has lots of fun
Jest swingin' its tail about,
But ef he opens his mouth, I run
'cause that's where the moo comes out.

"Recipe for a Happy Home"

If there was another passion in Mother's life—besides our father and poetry—it would have been food. She could remember the entire menu of any special dinner, even thirty or forty years before. Perhaps that's why she liked to recite "Recipe for a Happy Home."

Half a cup of friendship
    And a cup of thoughtfulness,

Creamed together with a pinch
    Of powdered tenderness.
Very lightly beaten
    In a cup of loyalty,
With a cup of faith and one of hope
    And one of charity.
Be sure to add a spoonful each
    Of gaiety that sings,
And also the ability
    To laugh at little things.
Moisten with sudden tears
    Of heartfelt sympathy.
Bake in a good-natured pan
    And serve repeatedly.

—*Author Unknown*

"Where's Mother?"

I used to think my father preached to us all the time—and my mother hardly ever. I now realize she preached to us *all* the time—but sneaked them by on the wings of a poem, like this one.

A little child from one to four,
I played near Mother on the floor;
But when she left the sitting room
To stir the fire or get the broom,
    I cried, "Where's Mother?"

When I was old enough to play
In the big front yard or new-mown hay,

I'd often run to the kitchen door
And call out loudly as before,
    "Where's Mother?"
When I was six, 'twas Mother's rule
To send me to the village school;
On my return you'd always hear,—
It made no difference who was near,—
    "Where's Mother?"

Then having grown beyond my teens,
I wandered on to other scenes;
But oft my footsteps I'd retrace,
Returning to the old home place,
    And call, "'Where's Mother?"

I entered then a larger life,
A field of struggle and of strife;
But oft returned, e'en as before,
To meet my sisters at the door,
    And cry, "Where's Mother?"

One day I knocked, but Mother slept
With peaceful smile; I turned and wept.
And now, alas! the dear "old farm"
To me has lost its greatest charm,—
    My mother.

When labor brings its well-earned rest,
If I awake among the blest
To see my Saviour in the sky,

I'm sure He'll hear me when I cry,
   "Dear Lord, where's Mother?"

                             —*Author Unknown*

"A SONG OF LIVING"

Finally, I have finished rummaging through Mother's scrapbooks. It strikes me that in her poetry is a wondrous philosophy of life, of what it means to be a mother—not just to her biological children but to the thousands of children of the spirit who called her "Mother." I am humbled by her drive, by her determination that her children would soar after leaving her nest. And they have: one is a composer, poet, and concert pianist; one is an artist; and the third is a writer.

All her life, Mother prepared us for her passing. In the "From the Cradle to the Grave" programs she and my father gave late in life, she would close with the one poem that summed up her passion for life: Amelia Burr's "A Song of Living." Interestingly enough, she first recited it at age fourteen in a high school elocutionary contest.

> Because I have loved life, I shall have no sorrow to die.
> I have sent up my gladness on wings to be lost in the blue
>   of the sky,
> I have run and leaped with the rain, I have taken the wind
>   to my breast.
> My cheek like a drowsy child to the face of the earth I have
>   pressed
> Because I have loved life, I shall have no sorrow to die.

I have kissed young love on the lips, I have heard his song
    to the end.
I have struck my hand like a seal, in the loyal hand of a friend,
I have known the peace of Heaven, the comfort of work
    done well.
I have longed for death in the darkness and risen alive out
    of Hell.
Because I have loved life, I have no sorrow to die.

I give a share of my soul to the world where my course is run.
I know that another shall finish the task that I leave undone.
I know that no flower, no flint, was in vain on the path I trod.
As one looks on a face through a window, through life, I
    have looked on God.
Because I have loved life, I shall have no sorrow to die.

THE DAY MOTHER CRIED

GERALD MOORE

Why is it that we think of our mother and father merely as pieces of the woodwork of our lives? Our parents merely dependable machines that we take for granted.

Gerald Moore remembers one day that changed his life: when he discovered his mother on the couch … crying.

Coming home from school that dark winter's day so long ago, I was filled with anticipation. I had a new issue of my favorite sports magazine tucked under my arm and the house to myself. Dad was at work, my sister was away, and Mother wouldn't be home from her new job for an hour. I bounded up the steps, burst into the living room and flipped on a light.

I was shocked into stillness by what I saw. Mother, pulled into a tight ball with her face in her hands, sat at the far end of the couch. She was crying. I had never seen her cry.

I approached cautiously and touched her shoulder. "Mother?" I said. "What's happened?"

She took a long breath and managed a weak smile. "It's nothing, really. Nothing important. Just that I'm going to lose this new job. I can't type fast enough."

"But you've only been there three days," I said. "You'll catch on." I was repeating a line she had spoken to me a hundred times when I was having trouble learning or doing something important to me.

"No," she said sadly. "There's no time for that. I can't carry my end of the load. I'm making everyone in the office work twice as hard."

"They're just giving you too much work," I said, hoping to find injustice where she saw failure. She was too honest to accept that.

"I always said I could do anything I set my mind to," she said. "And I still think I can in most things. But I can't do this."

I felt helpless and out of place. At age 16 I still assumed Mother could do anything. Some years before, when we sold our ranch and moved to town, Mother had decided to open a day nursery. She had had no training, but that didn't stand in her way. She sent away for correspondence courses in child care, did the lessons and in six months formally qualified herself for the task. It wasn't long before she had a full enrollment and a waiting list. Parents praised her, and the children proved by their reluctance to leave in the afternoon that she had won their affection. I accepted all this as a perfectly normal instance of Mother's ability.

But neither the nursery nor the motel my parents bought later had provided enough income to send my sister and me to college. I was a high school sophomore when we sold the motel. In two years I would be ready for college. In three more my sister would want to go. Time was running out, and Mother was frantic for ways to save money. It was clear that Dad could do no more than he was already doing—farming 80 acres in addition to holding a full-time job.

Looking back, I sometimes wonder how much help I deserved. Like many kids of 16, I wanted my parents' time and attention, but it never occurred to me that they might have needs and problems of their own. In fact, I understood nothing of their lives because I looked only at my own.

A few months after we'd sold the motel, Mother arrived home with a used typewriter. It skipped between certain letters and the keyboard was soft. At dinner that night I pronounced the machine a "piece of junk."

"That's all we can afford," Mother said. "It's good enough to learn on." And from that day on, as soon as the table was cleared and the dishes were done, Mother would disappear into her sewing room to practice. The slow tap, tap, tap went on some nights until midnight.

It was nearly Christmas when I heard her tell Dad one night that a good job was available at the radio station. "It would be such interesting work," she said. "But this typing isn't coming along very fast."

"If you want the job, go ask for it," Dad encouraged her.

I was not the least bit surprised, or impressed, when Mother got the job. But she was ecstatic.

Monday, after her first day at work, I could see that the excitement was gone. Mother looked tired and drawn. I responded by ignoring her.

Tuesday, Dad made dinner and cleaned the kitchen. Mother stayed in her sewing room, practicing. "Is Mother all right?" I asked Dad.

"She's having a little trouble with her typing," he said. "She needs to practice. I think she'd appreciate it if we all helped out a bit more."

"I already do a lot," I said, immediately on guard.

"I know you do," Dad said evenly. "And you may have to do more. You might just remember that she is working primarily so you can go to college."

I honestly didn't care. In a pique I called a friend and went out to get a soda. When I came home the house was dark, except for the band of light showing under Mother's door. It seemed to me that her typing had got even slower. I wished she would just forget the whole thing.

My shock and embarrassment at finding Mother in tears on Wednesday was a perfect index of how little I understood the pressures on her. Sitting beside her on the couch, I began very slowly to understand.

"I guess we all have to fail sometime," Mother said quietly. I could sense her pain and the tension of holding back the strong emotions that were interrupted by my arrival. Suddenly, something inside me turned. I reached out and put my arms around her.

She broke then. She put her face against my shoulder and sobbed. I held her close and didn't try to talk. I knew I was doing what I should, what I could, and that it was enough. In that moment, feeling Mother's back racked with emotion, I understood for the first time her vulnerability. She was still my mother, but she was something more: a person like me, capable of fear and hurt and failure. I could feel her pain as she must have felt mine on a thousand occasions when I had sought comfort in her arms.

Then it was over. Wiping away the tears, Mother stood and faced me. "Well, son, I may be a slow typist, but I'm not a parasite and I won't keep a job I can't do. I'm going to ask tomorrow if I can finish out the week. Then I'll resign."

And that's what she did. Her boss apologized to her, saying that he had underestimated his workload as badly as she had overestimated her typing ability. They parted with mutual respect, he offering a week's pay and she refusing it. A week later Mother took a job selling dry goods at half the salary the radio station had offered. "It's a job I can do," she said simply. But the evening practice sessions on the old green typewriter continued. I had a very different feeling now when I passed her door at night and heard her tapping away. I knew there was something more going on in there than a woman learning to type.

When I left for college two years later, Mother had an office job with better pay and more responsibility. I have to believe that in some strange way she learned as much from her moment of defeat as I did, because several years later, when I had finished school and proudly accepted a job as a newspaper reporter, she had already been a reporter with our hometown paper for six months.

Mother and I never spoke again about the afternoon when she broke down. But more than once, when I failed on a first attempt and was tempted by pride or frustration to scrap something I truly wanted, I would remember her selling dresses while she learned to type. In seeing her weakness I had not only learned to appreciate her strengths, I had discovered some of my own.

Not long ago, I helped Mother celebrate her 62nd birthday. I made dinner for my parents and cleaned up the kitchen afterward. Mother came in to visit while I worked, and I was reminded of the day years before when she had come home with that terrible old typewriter. "By the way," I said. "Whatever happened to that monster typewriter?"

"Oh, I still have it," she said. "It's a memento, you know . . . of the day you realized your mother was human. Things are a lot easier when people know you're human."

I had never guessed that she saw what happened to me that day. I laughed at myself. "Someday," I said, "I wish you would give me that machine."

"I will," she said, "but on one condition."

"What's that?"

"That you never have it fixed. It is nearly impossible to type on that machine, and that's the way it served this family best."

I smiled at the thought. "And another thing," she said. "Never put off hugging someone when you feel like it. You may miss the chance forever."

I put my arms around her and hugged her and felt a deep gratitude for that moment, for all the moments of joy she had given me over the years. "Happy birthday!" I said.

The old green typewriter sits in my office now, unrepaired. It *is* a memento, but what it recalls for me is not quite what it recalled for Mother. When I'm having trouble with a story and think about giving up, or when I start to feel sorry for myself and think things should be easier for me, I roll a piece of paper into that cranky old machine and type, word by painful word, just the way Mother did. What I remember then is not her failure, but her courage, the courage to go ahead.

It's the best memento anyone ever gave me.

THE LITTLEST ORPHAN AND THE CHRIST BABY

Margaret E. Sangster Jr.

The Littlest Orphan was cold and lonely—and the night was long. How he longed for someone to love—and someone to love him.

Then he had an idea.

he Littlest Orphan gazed up into the face of the Christ
Baby, who hung, gilt-framed and smiling, above the
mantel shelf. The mantel was dark, made of a black, mottled
marble that suggested tombstones, and the long room—despite
its rows of neat, white beds—gave an impression of darkness
too. But the picture above the mantel sparkled and scintillated
and threw off an aura of sheer happiness. Even the neat "In
Memoriam" card tacked to the wall directly under it could
not detract from its joy. All of rosy babyhood, all of unspoiled
laughter, all of the beginnings of life were in that picture! And
the Littlest Orphan sensed it, even though he did not quite
understand.

The Matron was coming down the room with many
wreaths, perhaps a dozen of them, braceleting her thin arm.
The wreaths were just a trifle dusty; their imitation holly
leaves spoke plaintively of successive years of hard usage. But
it was only two days before Christmas and the wreaths would
not show up so badly under artificial light. The board of
trustees, coming for the entertainment on Christmas Eve,
never arrived until the early winter dusk had settled down.
And the wreaths could be laid away, as soon as the holiday
was past, for another twelve months.

The Littlest Orphan, staring up at the picture, did not
hear the Matron's approaching footsteps. True, the Matron
wore rubber heels—but any other orphan in the whole asylum would have heard her. Only the Littlest Orphan, with
his thin, sensitive face and his curious fits of absorption,

could have ignored her coming. He started painfully as her sharp voice cut into the silence.

"John," she said, and the frost that made such pretty lace-work upon the window-pane wrought havoc with her voice. *"John, what are you doing here?"*

The Littlest Orphan answered after the manner of all small boy-children. "Nothin'!" he said.

Standing before him, the Matron—who was a large woman—seemed to tower. "You are not telling the truth, John," she said. "You have no right to be in the dormitory at this hour. Report to Miss Mace at once," (Miss Mace was the primary teacher) "and tell her that I said you were to write five pages in your copybook. *At once!*"

With hanging head the Littlest Orphan turned away. It seemed terribly unfair, although it was against the rules to spend any but sleeping hours in the dormitory! He was just learning to write, and five pages meant a whole afternoon of cramped fingers and tired eyes. But how could he explain to this grim woman that the Christ Baby fascinated him, charmed him, and comforted him? How could he explain that the Christ Baby's wide eyes had a way of glancing down, almost with understanding, into his own? How could he tell, with the few weak words of his vocabulary, that he loved the Christ Baby whose smile was so tenderly sweet? That he spent much of his time standing, as he stood now, in the shadow of that smile? He trudged away with never a word, down the length of the room, his clumsy shoes making a feeble clatter on the bare boards of the floor. When he was almost at the door, the Matron called after him.

"Don't drag your feet, John!" she commanded. And so he

walked the rest of the way on tiptoe. And closed the door very softly after him.

The halls had already been decorated with long streamers of red and green crepe paper that looped along, in a half-hearted fashion, from picture to picture. The stair railing was wound with more of the paper, and the schoolroom—where Miss Mace sat stiffly behind a broad desk—was vaguely brightened by red cloth poinsettias set here and there at random. But the color of them was not reflected in the Littlest Orphan's heart, as he delivered his message and received in return a battered copybook.

As he sat at his desk, writing laboriously about the cat who ate the rat and the dog who ran after the cat, he could hear the other orphans playing outside in the courtyard. Always they played from four o'clock—when school was over—until five-thirty, which was suppertime. It was a rule to play from four to five-thirty. They were running and shouting together—but in a stilted way. The Littlest Orphan did not envy them much. They were all older and stronger than he, and their games were sometimes hard to enjoy. He had been the last baby taken before a new ruling, making six years the minimum entrance age, had gone through. And he was only five years old now. Perhaps it was his very littleness that made the Matron more intolerant of him—he presented to her a problem that could not be met in a mass way. His clothing had to be several sizes smaller than the other clothing; his lessons less advanced. And so on.

Drearily he wrote. And listened, between sentences, to the scratching pen of Miss Mace . . . The dog had caught the cat. And now the man beat the dog. And then it was time to start all over again, back at the place where the cat ate the rat. Two pages, three pages, four pages . . . Surreptitiously the Littlest Orphan moved his fingers, one by one, and wondered that he was still able to move them. Then, working slowly, he finished the last page and handed the copybook back to the teacher. As she studied it, her face softened slightly.

"Why did the Matron punish you, John?" she asked, as if on impulse, as she made a correction in a sentence.

The Littlest Orphan hesitated for a second. And then: "I shouldn't have been in th' dormitory," he said slowly. "An' I was!"

Again Miss Mace asked a question.

"But what," she queried, "were you doing there? Why weren't you out playing with the other children?"

She didn't comment upon the fault, but the Littlest Orphan knew that she, also, thought the punishment rather severe. Only it isn't policy to criticize a superior's method of discipline. He answered her second question gravely.

"I was lookin' at th' Christ Baby over the mantel," he said.

As if to herself, Miss Mace spoke. "You mean the picture Mrs. Benchly gave in memory of her son," she murmured. "The pastel." And then, "Why were you looking at it—" She hesitated, and the Littlest Orphan didn't know that she had almost said "dear."

Shyly the child spoke, and wistfulness lay across his thin, small face—an unrealized wistfulness. "He looks so—nice," said the Littlest Orphan gently, "like he had a mother, maybe."

Supper that night was brief, and after supper there were carols to practice in the assembly room. The Littlest Orphan, seated at the extreme end of the line, enjoyed the singing. The red-headed boy, who fought so often in the court-yard, had a high, thrilling soprano. Listening to him, as he sang the solo parts, made the Littlest Orphan forget a certain black eye—and a nose that had once been swollen and bleeding. Made him forget lonely hours when he had lain uncomforted in his bed—as a punishment for quarreling.

The red-headed boy was singing something about "gold and frank-kin-sense, and myrrh." The Littlest Orphan told himself that they must be very beautiful things. Gold—the Christ Baby's frame was of gold—but frank-kin-sense and myrrh were unguessed names. Maybe they were flowers—real flowers that smelled pretty, not red cloth ones. He shut his eyes, singing automatically, and imagined what these flowers looked like—the color and shape of their petals, and whether they grew on tall lily stalks or on short pansy stems. And then the singing was over, and he opened his eyes with a start and realized that the Matron was speaking.

"Before you go to bed," she was saying, "I want you to understand that you must be on your good behavior until after the trustees leave tomorrow evening. You must not make any disorder in the corridors or in the dormitories—they have been especially cleaned and dusted. You must pay strict attention to the singing; the trustees like to hear you sing! They will all be here—even Mrs. Benchly, who has not visited us since her son died. And if one of you misbehaves—"

She stopped abruptly, but her silence was crowded with meaning, and many a child squirmed uncomfortably in his place. It was only after a moment that she spoke again.

"Good-night!" she said abruptly.

And the orphans chorused back, "Good-night."

Undressing carefully and swiftly, for the dormitory was cold and the gas lights were dim, the Littlest Orphan wondered about the trustees—and in particular about the Mrs. Benchly who had lost her son. All trustees were ogres to asylum children, but the Littlest Orphan couldn't help feeling that Mrs. Benchly was the least ogre-like of them all. Somehow she was a part of the Christ Baby's picture, and it was a part of her. If she were responsible for it, she could not be all bad! So ruminating, the Littlest Orphan said his brief prayers—any child who forgot his prayers was punished severely—and slid between the sheets into his bed.

Some orphans made a big lump under their bed covers. The red-headed boy was stocky, and so were others. Some of them were almost fat. But the Littlest Orphan made hardly any lump at all. The sheet, the cotton blanket, and the spread went over him with scarcely a ripple. Often the Littlest Orphan had wished that there might be another small boy who could share his bed—he took up such a tiny section of it. Another small boy would have made the bed seem warmer, somehow, and less lonely. Once two orphans had come to the asylum, and they were brothers. They had shared things—beds and desks and books. Maybe brothers were unusual gifts from a surprisingly blind providence, gifts that were granted only once in a hundred years! More rare, even, than mothers.

Mothers—the sound of the word had a strange effect upon

the Littlest Orphan, even when he said it silently in his soul. It meant so much that he did not comprehend—so much for which he vaguely hungered. Mothers stood for warm arms, and kisses, and soft words. Mothers meant punishments, too, but gentle punishment that did not really come from away inside.

Often the Littlest Orphan had heard the rest talking stealthily about mothers. Some of them could actually remember having owned one! But the Littlest Orphan could not remember. He had arrived at the asylum as a baby—delicate and frail and too young for memories that would later come to bless him and to cause a strange, sharp sort of hurt. When the rest spoke of bedtime stories, and lullabies, and sugar cookies, he listened—wide-eyed and half-incredulous—to their halting sentences.

It was growing very cold in the dormitory, and it was dark. Even the faint flicker of light had been taken away. The Littlest Orphan wiggled his toes, under the bottom blanket, and wished that sleep would come. Some nights it came quickly, but this night—perhaps he was overtired, and it was so cold!

As a matter of habit his eyes searched through the dark for the place where the Christ Baby hung. He could not distinguish even the dim outlines of the gilt frame, but he knew that the Christ Baby was rosy and chubby and smiling—that his eyes were deeply blue and filled with cheer. Involuntarily the Littlest Orphan stretched out his thin hands and dropped them back again against the spread. All about him the darkness lay like a smothering coat, and the Christ Baby, even though He smiled, was invisible. The other children were sleeping. All up and down the long room sounded their regular breathing, but the Littlest Orphan could not sleep. He wanted something that he was unable to define—wanted it with such a burning intensity that the tears crowded into his eyes. He sat up abruptly in his bed—a small, shivering figure with quivering lips and a baby ache in his soul that had never really known babyhood.

Loneliness—it swept about him. More disheartening than the cold. More enveloping that the darkness. There was no fear in him of the shadows in the corner, of the creaking shutters and the narrow stair. Such fears are discouraged early in children who live by rule and routine. No—it was a feeling more poignant than fear—a feeling that clutched at him and squeezed his small body until it was dry and shaking and void of expression.

Of all the sleeping dormitory the Littlest Orphan was the only child who knew the ache of such loneliness. Even the ones who had been torn away from family ties had, each one of them, something beautiful to keep preciously close. But the Littlest Orphan had nothing—nothing. . . . The loneliness filled him with a strange impulse, an impulse that sent him sliding over the edge of his bed with small arms outflung.

All at once he was crossing the floor on bare, mouse-quiet feet. Past the placidly sleeping children, past the row of lockers, past the table with its neat cloth and black-bound, impressive guest-book. Past everything until he stood, a white spot in the blackness, directly under the mantel. The Christ Baby hung above him. And, though the Littlest Orphan could not see, he felt that the blue eyes were looking down tenderly. All at once he wanted to touch the Christ Baby, to hold him tight, to feel the sweetness and warmth of him. Tensely, still moved by the curious impulse, he tiptoed back to where the table stood. Carefully he laid the guest-book on the floor; carefully he removed the white cloth. And then staggering under the—to him—great weight, he carried the table noiselessly back with him. Though it was really a small light table, the Littlest Orphan breathed hard as he set it down. He had to rest, panting, for a moment, before he could climb up on it.

All over the room lay silence, broken only by the sleepy sounds of the children. The Littlest Orphan listened almost prayerfully as he clambered upon the table top and drew himself to an erect position. His small hands groped along the mantel shelf, touched the lower edge of the gilt frame. But the Christ Baby was still out of reach.

Feverishly, obsessed with one idea, the Littlest Orphan raised himself on tiptoe. His hands gripped the chill marble of the mantel. Tugging, twisting—all with the utmost quiet—he pulled himself up until he was kneeling upon the mantel shelf. Quivering with nervousness as well as the now intense cold, he finally stood erect. And then—only then—he was able to feel the wire and nail that held the Christ Baby's frame against the wall. His numb fingers loosened the wire carefully. And then at last the picture was in his arms.

It was heavy, the picture. And hard. Not soft and warm as he had somehow expected it to be. But it was the Christ Baby nevertheless. Holding it close, the Littlest Orphan fell to speculating upon the ways of getting down, now that both of his hands were occupied. It would be hard to slide from the mantel to the table, and from table to floor, with neither sound nor mishap.

His eyes troubled, his mouth a wavering line in his pinched face, the Littlest Orphan crowded back against the wall. The darkness held now the vague menace of depth. Destruction lurked in a single misstep. It had been a long way up. It would be even longer going down. And he had the Christ Baby, as well as himself, to care for.

Gingerly he advanced one foot over the edge of the mantel—and drew it back. Sharply. He almost screamed in sudden terror. It was as if the dark had reached out long, bony fingers to pull him from his place of safety. He wanted to raise his hands to his face—but he could not release his hold upon the gilt frame. All at once he realized that his hands were growing numb with the cold and that his feet were numb, too.

The minutes dragged by. Somewhere a clock struck—many times. The Littlest Orphan had never heard the clock strike so many times, at night, before. He cowered back until it seemed to his scared, small mind that he would sink into the wall. And then, as the clock ceased striking, he heard another sound—a sound that brought dread to his heart. It was a step in the hall, a heavy, firm step that—despite rubber heels—was now clearly recognizable. It would be the Matron, making her rounds of the building before she went to bed. As the steps came nearer along the hall, a light, soft and yellow, seemed to glow in the place. It would be the lamp that she carried in her hand.

The Matron reached the door—peered in. And then, with lamp held high, she entered the room. And her swift glance swept the row of white beds—each, but one, with its sleeping occupant.

The Littlest Orphan, on the mantel, clutched the Christ Baby closer in his arms. And waited. It seemed to him that his shivering must shake the room. He gritted his teeth convulsively, as the Matron's eyes found his tumbled, empty bed.

Hastily, forgetting to be quiet, the woman crossed the room. She pulled back the spread, the blanket. And then—as if drawn by a magnet—her eyes lifted, travelled across the room. And found the small, white figure that pressed back into the narrow space. Her voice was sharper even than her eyes, when she spoke.

"John," she called abruptly—and her anger made her forget to be quiet—*"What are you doing up there?"*

Across the top of the Christ Baby's gilt frame, the eyes of the Littlest Orphan stared into the eyes of the Matron with something of the fascination that one sees in the eyes of a bird charmed by a cat or a snake. In narrow, white beds, all over the room, children were stirring, pulling themselves erect, staring. One child snickered behind a sheltering hand. But the Littlest Orphan was conscious only of the Matron. He waited for her to speak again. In a moment she did.

"John," she said, and her voice was burning, and yet chill, with rage, "you are a bad boy. *Come down at once!"*

His eyes blank with sheer fright, his arms clasping the picture close—the Littlest Orphan answered the tone of that voice. With quivering lips he advanced one foot, then the other. And stepped into the space that was the room below. He was conscious that some child screamed—he, himself, did not utter a sound. And that the Matron started forward. And then he struck the table and rolled with it, and the Christ Baby's splintering picture, into the darkness.

The Littlest Orphan spent the next day in bed, with an aching head and a wounded heart. The pain of his bruises did not make a great difference; neither did the threats of the Matron penetrate his consciousness. Only the bare space over the mantel mattered—only the blur of blue and yellow and red upon the hearth, where the pastel had struck. Only the knowledge that the Christ Baby—the meaning of all light and happiness—was no more, troubled him.

There was a pleasant stir about the asylum. An excited child, creeping into the dormitory, told the Littlest Orphan that one of the trustees had sent a tree. And that another was donating ice-cream. And that there were going to be presents. But the Littlest Orphan did not even smile. His wan face was set and drawn. Dire punishment waited him after his hurts were healed. And there would be no Christ Baby to go to for comfort and cheer when the punishment was over.

The morning dragged on. Miss Mace brought his luncheon of bread and milk and was as kind to him as she dared to be—your Miss Maces have been made timorous by a too forceful world. Once, during the early afternoon, the Matron came in to examine his bruised head, and once a maid came to rub the colored stains from the hearth. The Littlest Orphan caught his breath as he watched her. And then it began to grow dark, and the children were brought upstairs to be washed and dressed in clean clothes for the entertainment. They had been warned not to talk with him, and they obeyed—for there were folk watching and listening. But even so, flickers of conversation—excited, small-boy conversation—drifted to the Littlest Orphan's waiting ears. Someone had said there was to be a Santa Claus. In a red suit and a white beard. Perhaps—it was true. The Littlest Orphan slid down under the covers and pulled the sheet high over his aching head. He didn't want the rest to know that he was crying.

The face-washing was accomplished swiftly. Just as swiftly were the shirts adjusted to the last tie, string, and button. And then the children filed downstairs, and the Littlest Orphan was left alone again. He pulled himself up gingerly until he sat erect, and buried his face in his hands.

Suddenly, from downstairs, came the sound of music. First, the tiny piano, and then the voices of the children as they sang. Automatically the Littlest Orphan joined in, his voice quavering weakly through the empty place. He didn't want to sing—there was neither rhythm nor melody in his heart. But he had been taught to sing those songs, and sing them he must.

First, there was "O Little Town of Bethlehem." And then a carol. And then the one about "Gold and frank-kin-sense and myrrh." Strange that the words did not mean flowers tonight! And then there was a hush—perhaps it was a prayer. And then a burst of clapping and a jumble of glad cries. Perhaps that was the Santa Claus in his trappings of white and scarlet. The Littlest Orphan's tears came like hot rain to his tired eyes.

There was a sound in the hall. A rubber-heeled step on the bare floor. The Littlest Orphan slid down again under the covers, until only the bandage on the brow was at all visible. When the Matron stooped over him, she could not even glimpse his eyes. With a vigorous hand she jerked aside the covers.

"Sick or not," she told him, "you've got to come downstairs. Mrs. Benchly wants to see the boy who broke her son's memorial picture. I'll help you with your clothes."

Trembling violently, the Littlest Orphan allowed himself to be wedged into shorts and a shirt and a pair of coarse, dark trousers. He laced his shoes with fingers that shook with mingled fear and weakness. And then he followed the Matron out of the dormitory and through the long halls, with their mocking festoons of red and green crepe paper, and into the assembly room where the lights were blinding and the Christmas tree was a blaze of glory.

The trustees sat at one end of the room, the far end. They were a mass of dark colors, blacks and browns and somber grays. Following in the wake of the Matron, the Littlest Orphan stumbled toward them. Mrs. Benchly—would she beat him in front of all the rest? Would she leap at him accusingly from that dark mass? He felt smaller than he had ever felt before, and more inadequate.

The children were beginning to sing again. But despite their singing, the Matron spoke. Not loudly, as she did to the children, but with a curious deference.

"This is John, Mrs. Benchly," she said, "the child who broke the picture."

Biting his lips, so that he would not cry out, the Littlest Orphan stood in the vast shadow of the Matron. He shut his eyes. Perhaps if this Mrs. Benchly meant to strike him, it would be best to have his eyes shut. And then suddenly a voice came, a voice so soft that somehow he could almost feel the velvet texture of it.

"Poor child," said the voice, "he's frightened. And ill, too. Come here, John. I won't hurt you, dear."

Opening his eyes incredulously, the Littlest Orphan stared past the Matron into the sort of face small children dream about. Violet-eyed and tender. Lined, perhaps, and sad about the mouth, and wistful. But so sweet! Graying hair, with a bit of wave in it, brushed back from a broad, white brow. And slim, white, reaching hands. The Littlest Orphan went forward without hesitation. Something about this lady was reminiscent of the Christ Baby. As her white hand touched his, tightened on it, he looked up into her face with the ghost of a smile.

The children had crowded almost informally to the other end of the room, toward the tree. The dark mass of the trustees was dissolving, breaking up into fragments, that followed the children. One of the trustees laughed aloud. Not at all like an ogre. A sudden sense of gladness began—for no understandable reason—to steal across the Littlest Orphan's consciousness. Rudely the voice of the Matron broke in upon it.

"I had warned the children," she said, "not to disturb anything. Last evening, before they retired, John deliberately disobeyed. And the picture is ruined in consequence. What do you think we had better do about it, Mrs. Benchly?"

For a moment the lady with the dream face did not speak. She was drawing the Littlest Orphan nearer, until he touched the satin folds of her black gown, and despite the Matron's voice, he was not afraid. When at last she answered the Matron, he did not flinch.

"I think," she said gently, "that I'll ask you to leave us. I would like to talk with John—alone."

As the Matron walked stiffly away, down the length of the room, she lifted the Littlest Orphan into her lap.

"I know," she said, and her voice was even gentler than it had been, "that you didn't mean to break the picture. Did you, dear?"

Eagerly the Littlest Orphan answered, "Oh, no—ma'am!" he told her. "I didn't mean t' break th' Christ Baby."

The woman's arms were about him. They tightened suddenly. "You're so young," she said; "you're such a mite of a thing. I doubt if you could understand why I had the picture made. Why I gave it to the home here to be hung in the dormitory. . . . My little son was all I had after my husband died. And his nursery—it was such a pretty room—had a Christ Child picture on the wall. And my boy always loved the picture. . . . And so when he—left—" her voice faltered, "I had an artist copy it. I—I couldn't part with the original! And I sent it to a place where there would be many small boys, who could enjoy it as my son had always—" Her voice broke.

The Littlest Orphan stared in surprise at the lady's face. Her violet eyes were misted like April blossoms with the dew upon them. Her lips quivered. Could it be that she, too, was lonesome and afraid? His hand crept up until it touched her soft cheek.

"I *loved* th' Christ Baby," he said simply.

The lady looked at him. With an effort she downed the quaver in her voice. "I can't believe," she said at last, "that you destroyed the picture purposely. No matter what she"—her glance rested upon the Matron's stiff figure, half a room away—"may think! John, dear, did you mean to spoil the gift I gave—in my small boy's name? Oh—I'm sure you didn't."

All day long the Littlest Orphan had lived in fear and agony of soul. All day long he had known pain—physical pain and the pain of suspense. Suddenly he buried his face in the lady's neck—he had never known before that there was a place in ladies' necks, just made for tiny heads—and the tears came. Choked by sobs, he spoke.

"No'm," he sobbed, "I didn't mean to. . . . It was only

because I was cold. And lonesome. And th' bed was—big. An'
all th' rest was asleep. An' the Christ Baby always looked so
pink . . . an' glad . . . an' warm. An' I wanted t' take him inter
my bed. An' cuddle close!"—he burrowed his head deeper into
the neck—"so that I wouldn't be cold any more. Or lonesome—any more."

The lady's arms tightened about the Littlest Orphan's
body until the pressure almost hurt—but it was a nice sort
of hurt. It shocked her, somehow, to feel the thinness of that
body. And her tears fell quite unrestrained upon the Littlest
Orphan's bandaged head. And then all at once she bent over.
And her lips pressed, ever so tenderly, upon the place where
his cheek almost met her ear.

"Not to be cold," she whispered, more to herself than to
the Littlest Orphan, "or lonesome any more! To have the nursery opened again—and the sound of the tiny feet in the empty
rooms. To have the Christ Child smiling down upon a sleeping little boy. To kiss bruises away again . . . Not to be lonesome any more, or cold—"

Suddenly she tilted back the Littlest Orphan's head; was
looking deep, deep into his bewildered eyes.

"John," she said, and his name sounded so different
when she said it—"how would you like to come away from
here, and live in my house, with me? How would you like
to be my boy?"

A silence had crept over the other end of the room. One
of the trustees, who wore a clerical collar, had mounted the
platform. He was reading from the Bible that visiting minis-
ters read from of a Sunday. His voice rang—resonant and rich
as an organ tone—through the room.

"For unto us a child is born," he read, *"unto us a son is given."*

The Littlest Orphan, with a sign of utter happiness, crowded closer into the arms that held him.

And it was Christmas Eve!

THE MUSTARD PLASTER

AUTHOR UNKNOWN

In days gone by, it was felt that colds could be conquered by the application of mustard plasters. Unfortunately for the patient who stood between the mustard plaster and the cold, the remedy was worse than the cold—far, far worse!

Bobby Dryenforth had a cold that threatened to settle on his lungs. Mrs. Dryenforth knew that he ought to have a mustard plaster, but the question was how to get it on him. Bobby did not like medicine. Most boys don't. He'd never heard of a mustard plaster, but if he *had* been told that it was for him he would probably have run away and gone swimming. Mrs. Dryenforth went quietly down to the store and bought a box of English mustard and then had it wrapped up in about a dozen sheets of different colored paper and brought it home. With great deliberation she unwrapped it in the presence of Bobby and his younger brother Phil. "What is it?" both boys cried in chorus.

"It is genuine English mustard," she said impressively.

"What's it good for?" inquired Bobby.

"It is a great luxury, my son, and it makes the best mustard plasters in the world."

"Oh say, Mother, will you make us one right away and show us?"

Mrs. Dryenforth slowly and carefully wrapped the mustard again in the colored paper. The boys looked disappointed. They besought her to make one even if she kept it all to herself and didn't give them one bit of it.

"I'll tell you what. I'll make one tonight and whichever one has been the best boy today shall take it to bed with him tonight."

Having made this offer she adjusted her spectacles and the goodness began to shine out from the skins of those boys.

They grew better and better all afternoon. She sent Phil out after a pail of water and Bobby ran out and took it away from him to get the credit for the deed. They brought in wood enough to last three winters. In fact if merit alone would win mustard plasters they both deserved to be covered from head to floor with them. The rivalry was very interesting while it lasted. But there was one moment during the day when Bobby could have sold his chances at a very low figure. This was at supper. The Rev. Kimmerly was a guest. Something always happens when a boy is trying to be good. Bobby's virtue was wrecked on . . . the last piece of cake on the plate.

But he thought of the mustard plaster and would not yield. Presently he thought compromise.

Pass the plate around, said a familiar voice inside his conscience. *If nobody takes it, then you can have it.* So Bobby made a circuit. Every adult refused it—Bobby hesitated.

"Brother Phil," he said in an affectionate tone, but with a look which meant, *If you take it, I'll lick you tomorrow*— "Brother Phil, will you have a piece of cake?"

"Don't care if I do," said Phil, and grabbed it. That was when the plaster ceased to attract Bobby. He raised the plate as high as he could wave it in the air. "Horrid old thing!" he cried. Then he cast the plate down with a crash on the floor and ran out of the room.

At 9:30 the boys were put to bed. Mrs. Dryenforth then compounded the plaster. Phil watched her with a smile of conscious rectitude; Bobby through a mist of tears.

"Bobby," said Mother, "You have been a naughty boy and almost broke the plate—and you have sworn in the presence of the minister." Bobby groaned, and Phil chuckled. "But

Phil," continued the just judge, "has been the worst. He knew that you wanted that cake and should have let you have it. He tempted you to do what you did. The plaster therefore goes to Bobby."

Phil gasped and Bobby almost jumped out of bed. "This may feel a little chilly at first but that will soon pass," said Mother as she securely tied the strings where he could not get hold of them.

Phil tried to pretend that he was asleep to conceal his envy but at last curiosity got the better of him. "Is it chilly now, Bobby?" he whispered. "No, it's got over that now. Mother said it would." After another considerable lapse of silence, "Mother," said Bobby, "I would be willing to give the plaster to Phil. I feel mean about keeping it all to myself."

"No, you have won it fairly, Bobby, and you shall have it all."

"But I've had it a long time," said Bobby.

"Suppose I let Phil take it for a while. Say a couple of hours or so?"

"No, that wouldn't be fair. Go to sleep now, boys, perhaps some day I'll make one for Phil."

"Why don't you make one for him *now*? There's plenty of mustard." But Mother did not reply.

Phil, meanwhile, in view of his brother's generosity, began to forgive him for being better than he.

"Mother," said Bobby.

"Tell me about it tomorrow," she said.

"But Mother, perhaps I've not been as good as you thought I've been." He confessed two or three minor frailties, but they had no effect. Finally, he invented a fearful crime of which he had been entirely innocent. It didn't work either.

"I say, Bobby, what's come over you," said Phil. "Don't you feel well?"

"My conscience hurts me," said Bobby, shifting around in bed trying to get the plaster in a cool place.

"You aren't going to die, are you, Bobby?"

"I don't know," said Bobby. And he truly didn't know. "If you really feel bad about it I can untie the strings. Turn over— I'll untie them—"

No sooner said than done. Then Bobby adjusted the plaster in a like manner that experience most grievous had taught him and tied the strings in such a manner that it would take a surgical operation to get the burning mass off of Phil's chest.

"Good night, Mother. I think I'll go to sleep now. The plaster doesn't burn as much as it did."

Presently Bobby felt a vigorous kick. "Bobby, you pirate, get this thing off of me before I do something terrible."

"You asked me for it and you'll keep it." Another pause during which Phil experimented with the strings unsuccessfully.

"I'll tell Mother," he whispered.

"You don't dare. She'll make it warmer for you than plaster."

Half an hour later, Mrs. Dryenforth cautiously approached the bed. Bobby was asleep but Phil lay on his back with tears trickling down his face.

"Poor little Phil," she said, kissing him. "Don't feel badly. I'll make you one some day.

"No, Mother, you needn't. I can get along quite nicely without it."

THE SONG OF SONGS

MABEL MCKEE

Dr. and Mrs. Dean tried to make the best of it, but it was so difficult. Neither David nor Eleanor showed any signs of coming home. Not even on Mother's Day.

But Mother Dean had one last arrow in her quiver, and it shot to its target, marked "Special Delivery."

When Eleanor Dean did not come home at Christmas time, people at Libertyville began to shake their heads and say to one another, "She is going to be exactly like David. Dr. and Mrs. Dean have lost not only their son, but their daughter as well."

But Mother Dean, who had bravely crushed her longing for her only daughter in order that she might have an opportunity to do the work she wanted to do, as had David, who the year before had graduated from a medical college, again put away her own grief and comforted Dr. Dean. "She'll come home in the springtime," she promised, "and sing in the choir so every one can hear how her voice has improved under this study. After all, it takes time to come from Cincinnati to western Indiana, and no doubt she has some important engagement to sing in a Christmas choir."

Spring brought another letter from Eleanor. It read: "Mother dear, I know you'll understand how grieved I am to have to tell you I cannot leave my work now even for just a few days. But soon, very soon, I hope I'll be coming home."

Father's face had grown grave. "It seems as if our children have no more time for us, dear," he murmured. "Our neighbors were right when they said that if we let them go too far away to be educated, they would grow away from us."

Mother's eyes were dim with tears. But courage in her heart made her whisper: "I'm not going to let them grow away from me. I shall write and tell them both they must come home for Mother's Day. Eleanor never has been away from me on a single Mother's Day. She'll come, I'm sure."

Eleanor, though, just eighteen, was "still a baby" down in Mrs. Dean's heart. When David went away to college, Eleanor was only ten, and then she wept bitter tears. "Davie won't ever come home just Davie."

"Oh, yes, he will," Mrs. Dean had comforted. "He'll graduate from college and medical school. Then when he comes home for good, he'll put up a sign on the door of Father's office with his name on it, and folks will speak of them as 'The two Doctors Dean.'"

"But he'll be different then," she had persisted. "He won't love me then as he does now."

David's arms had gone around her. "Why, little sister, do you think I ever could forget you? If ever you would call and I were in the middle of the ocean, I'd still come to you."

Eleanor, a slender little girl with masses of golden curls and big blue eyes, had slipped off her brother's knee and gone to her beloved piano. Softly touching some chords, she had sung, "Love goes on forever, I shall not forget."

David's eyes had suddenly filled with tears, though he was as tall as his father and called himself a man. When a small boy his mother had taught him the words of that beautiful Norwegian folk song, "Mother Dear." He in turn had taught it to Eleanor.

> *Mother, mother dear! When night is near,*
> *When the ruddy sun is sinking,*
> *Then your loving care makes a tender prayer;*
> *Then of me your heart is thinking.*

And he had told his mother then, "Eleanor is going to be a beautiful singer someday. I have never seen a child who could carry a tune as she does."

While David was away at college, Eleanor finished the lower grades and went to high school. She played the piano for the high school orchestra; she sang in the girls' glee club, and whenever the school gave an operetta, Eleanor Dean always had the leading part. Dr. and Mrs. Dean dreamed of a time when David would be home again, his father's assistant, and Eleanor would be the soloist in the church choir; when she would direct cantatas and sing the leading part in community oratorios.

After Eleanor graduated from high school, she begged her parents for just a year at the conservatory. Her teachers told her that she could earn part of her expenses there by singing in church choirs and teaching a few pupils. She knew that her parents had pinched and saved to educate David; so she would take from them only enough money to transport her to Cincinnati and keep her there the first few months.

"I'll come home every few weeks, Mother dear," she had promised when she went away. "Every few weeks!"

Now it would soon be a year since she left, and Eleanor had made only one trip home, and that had been the third week after she had left. It was just a week before Mother's Day when a letter came to the Dean home, saying: "It breaks my heart to disappoint you, Mother, but again I find I can't get away. So you'll have to have Mother's Day without me. I'm going to take a vacation in June or July, and then I'll surely come. And I'll be thinking of you every minute on that day, Mother. Don't forget that."

Mrs. Dean dropped down beside her little sewing table

and sobbed. Dr. Dean, who had seldom seen his wife break down like this, went over to her and put his arms around her. He had known stories like this one they were living—stories in which children forgot the parents who had sacrificed for them. But this in reality—oh, this seemed ten times more bitter than any of the stories he had read.

They had grown used to David's being away from home over the different holidays. College was too far away for him to come. When he was awarded his diploma from medical college, the president there explained to Dr. Dean that another year's hospital work would do much for his son. That delayed David's homecoming, but the Deans had stood it. And now it was May, and he was to come home in June to stay, according to the plans that he and his father had made years before.

But Mother Dean was sad. "It is Eleanor my heart is hungry for. I didn't think she would so completely fail me."

The little living room in which she had read and sung to both her children grew inexpressibly dear to her then. She wiped her eyes and looked around it. There were the photographs of Eleanor. The little cuckoo clock had been a gift from David, bought with the first money he earned running errands.

Eleanor had hemmed the drapes for the window and made the fluffy pillows on the couch. She had re-enameled the frame of grandmother's picture to match the rich maroon tones in the paper. She had chosen the rugs and the upholstered wicker suite by taking some scraps of the wallpaper to the store.

Why, Eleanor is a little homemaker, she thought to herself. *If only she had not had such a rare voice she would be at home with us and doubly happy, I'm sure. I remember now how she used to tiptoe to the piano and sing.*

Like a dream from the land of yesterday there came directly before her the vision of a little girl and boy standing close beside her at the piano as she played. They were singing in their childish voices, so sweetly and lovingly, that old Norwegian song:

> *Mother, mother dear! When the day is here,*
> *While you count the hours without me,*
> *Then your tender heart thinks of me apart,*
> *Still you dream about me.*

A quick smile came to her lips. Not only had memory brought it there, but a sudden inspiration as well. She waited until Dr. Dean had started to his office, and then she began a search through the bookcases and closets for an old music book, the one which contained "The Song of Songs," as David had called it. She was going to tear that leaf from the book and send it to Eleanor.

It will bring her home if anything can, she told herself hopefully. *I mustn't tell Father. He'll think I'm taking an unfair advantage. But he doesn't understand. He is sure of David's return in a few weeks' time. But right now I'm not sure that Eleanor even wants to come home; so I'm going to call her.*

I'd rather have her here to love than to have all the fame and fortune she might win if she stays away for years and studies. Nothing else matters in the land of happiness but love.

Up in the luxurious fraternity house near a big Chicago hospital, two young men and an older one were talking at that very minute. All three were physicians. Dr. Lieber, the older one, was from a town far north in Wisconsin, where he had a noted clinic. He had come down to Chicago to find two promising young men to train as assistants. The fame of his clinic was so great that when he had trained his assistants, he was always losing them to city surgeons for younger partners.

He suddenly placed his hand on the arm of one of the younger men. "Dean," he said persuasively, "the surgeons here say that you will do well as a specialist. I feel that I can help you; besides, you can be of great service to me. I'm willing to increase the salary I offered you if you are interested in my proposition."

David Dean hesitated. His chum, Paul Hylton, who had already accepted an offer from the physician, reached out and clasped his other hand. "Of course you'll go, Dave," he coaxed. "You must not go back to that sleepy little hometown of yours and hide your talents under a bushel. You must go where you will have the best opportunity."

Still David hesitated. He seemed to hear his father say: *The sick people of a small town and country district are entitled to as good doctors and teachers as those in crowded cities. Fame will come to a great man no matter where he is.*

Too, he seemed to see Mother and a sad face and tears in her eyes—homesick for him and Eleanor. At times his heart held a feeling of sorrow because Eleanor thought fame came ahead of happiness and because she was away from home.

Then like a flash from the land of yesterday there came into his memory Eleanor's letters, which had begun to tell of her loneliness in Cincinnati. Sometimes she hinted of going home, and always then he had written her, "Buck up, Eleanor. Success is always purchased by hard work and loneliness."

Tonight he wondered if that were true. His father was successful, according to many people, yet he had stayed among the people he loved—in a small town. He turned to Dr. Lieber. "I can't decide just yet," he said. "I must find out whether my father is really well and if he needs me. Give me a week to find out. I'll telegraph you then. If I decide to come, I'll be there at the same time Hylton is."

Back in the small bachelor apartment that he and Paul Hylton shared, the two of them talked over the surgeon's offer. David listened to his chum tell of the great opportunity ahead of the man who specialized, so long as he stayed in a great city. At the same time he thought of his father's hard life, caring for men injured in mine accidents, bringing tiny babies into the world, often acting as spiritual guide as well as body physician. Yet, with all this, Father seemed much happier than most of the men whom he knew.

While he sat thinking, Paul went to the radio he had recently bought, and was tuning in on a distant station for the concert he tried to get every evening. As he worked the dials, he murmured, "I wish you liked music as I do, Dave. We'd have the radio on all the time and study to music."

David didn't even hear him. To himself he was saying, *I wish something big and vital would happen to help me decide this proposition. It is entirely too big for me.*

Mother's letter to Eleanor, bearing the little song of yesterday, had gone by special delivery. It was on the hall table in her boarding house when she reached home that evening. When she saw the envelope, Eleanor made a dash for it, almost break- ing, in her haste, the beautiful little Wedgewood pitcher she had just bought for Mother with her savings, because she thought it was the prettiest Mother's Day gift she could find.

She opened the envelope. Mother often sent her letters by special delivery, so Eleanor was not afraid that it was a message of sickness or trouble. She expectantly slipped in her fingers and drew out the piece of music. "Oh," she cried in a disap- pointed tone, to her chum, "Mother is getting absent-minded, and forgot to put her letter in with this clipping."

Half-heartedly she unfolded the sheet of music, along the edges of which were the marks of little thumbs that had touched it when she and David were tiny. Rather curiously she glanced at the page. Listlessly she read the first line:

> *Mother, mother dear!*
> *When the night is near.*

She stopped short. Tears rushed to her eyes, and she began to cry softly, while Elsie (her chum), carrying the pre- cious pitcher in her own hand, helped her up the stairway to their room.

There Eleanor told Elsie what message that song had brought to her. Mother Dean didn't believe she wanted to come home for Mother's Day. Mother still thought she was a success, and that leaving the city for a few days could be man- aged as easily as if she were in her own town (the little song had been sent to remind her), while she, still a failure, just couldn't go home to admit her defeat. When she had found some kind of success, then she could go home with her head held high, and then they would be proud of her.

Eleanor's heart had almost broken with grief when she learned from the teachers at the conservatory that she had just a sweet voice, not strong enough for concert work. She had thought of how ashamed the people at home would be if she went home and told them that she would never bring them fame as all the newspapers had predicted at the time of her graduation.

Then she had decided to win success as a pianist. Not one word about her disappointment did she write home. And when her little supply of money was used up taking lessons; she did what hundreds of other girls at that time were doing— she went searching for work to help pay her expenses.

After days of fruitless searching for a job she had found work at the music counter of a five-and-ten-cent store. There she met Elsie, who also had determined to climb higher, and soon the two girls were rooming together. Elsie had gotten her "on" in the chorus with which she sometimes sang at a radio broadcasting station. It added to their income, and it made possible the little Wedgewood pitcher and other gifts Eleanor was sending home.

"I don't see how I can sing tonight," Eleanor sobbed. "When I think of Mother alone at home, with her heart aching, I just can't sing a note."

Elsie patted her on the shoulder, at the same time imploring her to hurry. "Nan goes on at seven," she coaxed. "If she hadn't been sick, they never would have given you a chance to sing a solo. It's your chance to get home, honey. Can't you see that? It will not be regarded as a failure in your town to be a soloist at a broadcasting station."

Eleanor laughed shakily through her tears. "I'm soloist for just one night as a substitute," she reminded her.

By the time they left the house for the broadcasting station, Eleanor was laughing. She was going to sing three popular numbers that Nan had sent her.

Folded in Eleanor's purse when she entered the room was the envelope which had brought grief to her earlier in the evening. She had quite forgotten it, however, until the announcer, glancing through the music she had placed on the piano, said, "I wish Nan had given you 'Mother Machree' or something like it. Several of our listeners-in have already asked for mother songs because Mother's Day is so near."

Eleanor took the song from her purse and unfolded it. "Why, I have a mother's song here," she said. "If you like it, I'll sing it. And please announce that it is being sung especially for Dr. and Mrs. Dean of Libertyville, Indiana, by their daughter."

Then when the time came, the little Norwegian folk song she had always loved so dearly rang out its message on the air:

Then your loving care makes a tender prayer.

When Paul Hylton tuned in on a dinner-hour concert, David Dean rather impatiently said, "Can't endure those Italian songs any longer. Guess I'll take a walk while you listen to that."

He had just got his hat, when Paul ran out of the door after him. "There's a song being sung to Dr. and Mrs. Dean, of Libertyville," he said excitedly. "That's your father and mother, isn't it?"

Almost immediately a sweet, girlish voice came singing through the air,

Mother, dear mother!
      When night is near.

David dropped down in front of the radio set, his head resting in his hand while he listened:

Mother, mother dear!
      Whether far or near,
Well I know you'll never fail me.
      Mother love will be
Ever near to me.
      When the bitter days assail me;
Love goes on forever,
      I shall not forget.

He jumped up when it was done. "That is my sister singing," he said. "I could hear her crying in that song. Something is wrong. She is more homesick than her letters indicated. Paul, I am going after her tonight, and I don't think I'll go to Dr. Lieber's clinic with you. I know I won't until I have been home to see if Father needs me."

Mother's Day found Mother Dean without a gift except Father's flowers. Of course it was only seven o'clock when they sat down at the breakfast table together, and a special delivery boy could come at any time, but still she had a feeling that her children had forgotten this day of days of hers.

She tried to be very cheerful, so Father would not notice the absence of gifts from their children. She gaily reminded him that there was maple syrup to eat with the waffles, but it required a good deal of courage to keep the tears out of her voice. It would have been much easier if she could have cried out her grief on his shoulder.

As she began to butter her first cake, there was a sound of footsteps on the back porch, just as there had been in the old days when her children came home from school together. With a quick jerk the outside door was opened, and David and Eleanor were rushing into the room. Together they laughed and cried, "Mother, dear! Dad, you darling!"

For a few minutes Mother held them in her arms, murmuring foolish nothings, all the while trying to listen while they explained they were late because Eleanor had to pack her things to bring home. She had come to stay. And if Dr. Dad wanted him, David was ready to enter his office and take old Mrs. Lankford and some of the rest of his chronic patients off his hands. Mother laughed and cried over them while she asked herself in her heart, *What was wrong with my faith as I prayed for them to come?*

Now that they were here, Mother fairly flew to the kitchen for some more waffles and to breathe a prayer of thankfulness to God for bringing them back even while she had doubted. When she returned to the table, the bouquet of sweetheart roses that David had bought at the florist's shop down the street and the little Wedgewood pitcher were beside her plate, and on them was a card with the message she never, never could forget.

"Love goes on forever, I shall not forget."

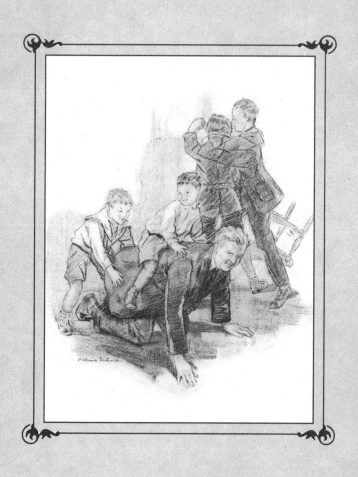

THIRD TIME'S THE CHARM

KATHERINE HOLLAND BROWN

unty was troubled. Now that their five children were grown, now that they'd gotten the travel bug out of their system, now that they'd once again reached a peak of health—well, they just missed a house full of children.

So she did something about it.

But . . . Lord have mercy! Even that wasn't enough.

"Heard the news?" shrilled my friend Sophie Curtis, over the phone. "The Uncle Jimmy Garrettsons have gone and started on another set of children! Five, this time. His niece's sister-in-law's, I think. Or else his sister-in-law's niece's. And Uncle Jimmy past sixty, and Aunty fifty-eight! Of all the reckless performances—"

"Reckless fiddlesticks," I called back.

Yes, I'll admit that the Uncle Jimmy Garrettsons have certainly done their duty in life, and more. To have brought up two sets of children seems task enough for one man and wife. But if ever two human beings were ordained by Heaven to be father and mother to every lonely little waif that wanders by, those two are the Garrettsons. True, they're getting on in years, but they have every tool for the art of life: health, deep mutual affection, kindly wisdom, and money. And don't imagine for a moment that they've let themselves be tied down. They're no doormat parents. Not they.

Of course, their own children were a pretty stiff proposition. Five of them, three boys and two girls: superb children, but reckless, headstrong, young whirlwinds, every one. To borrow the candid phrase of the oldest town habitant, the three boys promised for a while to turn out gallows meat. They were always up to mischief, exasperating and dangerous mischief, at that. They were always starting something that Uncle Jimmy had to finish. The year that his two beautiful, self-willed daughters were carrying on so tempestuously, Uncle Jimmy got to looking mighty haggard and drawn, for so young and prosperous a man. And that time the two boys were both expelled from high-school, Aunty's pink cheeks whitened and dark shadows filled her kind, gentle eyes.

But, at last, all five had scrambled and stumbled up Fools' Hill—to quote the oldest habitant again. And in justice let it be said that all five turned out splendidly. The girls married happily and well, the boys pitched into business with as much clean hilarious vim as they had pitched into football, not three years before. And Uncle Jimmy drew a long breath: then he gathered up Aunty, and took her to Europe for a long, gorgeous, restful year.

They came back, looking ten years younger, bubbling with health and pep and enthusiasm, their trunks stuffed with goodies for everybody in town. But after a few weeks all that sparkle and good cheer seemed to fade.

"We've got everything in the world to make us happy," said Aunty, sadly, to me. "We're well and strong, and we have our home, and our friends, and everything we can ask for. Everything—and nothing. For—we're just starved for children."

"Starved for children—" I gulped.

"Of course we've five of our own. But they're all grown up, and off they've gone to live their own lives. So we haven't a thing to do. And Papa's fifty—that isn't really old. And I'm forty-six. We ought to be enjoying every minute. Instead—"

She broke off, and glanced down the long garden. Uncle Jimmy was coming slowly up the path. In those three weeks at home, Uncle Jimmy had—well, slumped. Slumped, from the weary sag of his fine gray head to both dragging, discouraged feet. Still a handsome man, stout and florid, almost too stout and florid, in truth, yet he was the picture of a creature despondent to the heart.

"What under the sun," said I, anxiously.

"Oh, he isn't sick. Though he looks as if he'd been tramped on by all the woes that ever trod shoe leather. He's just blue."

"If he had a new interest," I ventured.

"He's going to have a new interest. We're going to adopt a whole family. Next week."

I gulped again. Leave it to Aunty!

"I know him so well. I know that only children will content him." Her loving eyes bent on him tenderly. "And—" she went on, with her quaint serenity, "it seems almost providential that I just heard of the little Mathews boys, over at Riverview. Their mother died last year, and their father has just deserted them, poor babies. Four boys, two years apart—little steps, just like our own." Then, suddenly, her old radiance came shining back. "Yes, it's all settled. They'll come Monday. Oh, Papa doesn't know it yet. I'm saving it for a surprise."

The little Mathews boys came, and they filled Uncle's lonely heart to the brim. Filled his hands, too. They were almost as rambunctious a clan as were the five that preceded them. Four of them, mind you. From Bobby, fourteen, down to John Calvin, eight, they were one perennial riot. Many a time did the oldest town inhabitant vow that Uncle had no business keeping those young ripsnorters cooped up in a civilized town.

They ought to be turned loose on a large island, surrounded by a larger ocean. But they came through, all right, and, in no time at all, they were the town's pride and glory. But by that time Uncle's thick crest was gray in good earnest, and Aunty's placid brow knew several new lines.

With Bobby through Tech, and married to the finest girl in the world, and John Calvin a sophomore under the watchful eyes of two firm elder brothers, Uncle and Aunty went for another trip—a long one. When they came back from that journey, Aunty could tell you all about the perfumes, so-called, of Samar-Kand, and how Papa got pinched for speeding in Peking; and Uncle, with the face of a contented boy, could describe the moonrise over Istanbul, and how Mamma got short-changed buying sandalwood fans in Cairo. They'd had the time of their young lives, and their two sets of children, who had missed them unspeakably, nearly ate them up. But after the first glow of home-coming had dimmed, I caught a wistful look, now and then. And I wondered how they would fill the years that remained to them. And now, behold, the niece's sister-in-law had furnished the solution.

An hour after Sophie had telephoned me, I met Uncle in Sandro's fruit market. Uncle, his old gay confident self, all cheery and brisk and beaming.

"Yes, Sophie told you correctly. Remarkable woman, Sophie. Mother and I made our decision only this morning. Mother phoned Sophie at approximately 9:40 a.m. By this time I'll wager the entire town knows our plans, and has talked them over. Yes, three boys. Our third try at raising a crop of boys. And believe me, Louise, this time Mamma and I are going to take a new tack. We—we feel that this family must cost us less in—in—well, in several ways—than our other two families cost. So we're going to break up our place here, and move. To the country."

◯◯

Move to the country! Break up that dignified, luxurious home, at their time of life!

"Yes. No, we're not going for reasons of economy. Nor for fresh air. Nor for any other reason that you'd guess. We're going where we can find—chores."

"*Chores!*

"Yes, chores. C-H-O-R-E-S. According to Webster, a piece of minor domestic work, as about a house or barn, of regular and frequent occurrence. Small steady jobs, that demand promptness, and accuracy, and regular hours. D'you get me?"

"Why, you never asked your own boys to do one thing at home. And your girls didn't make their own beds, even. And the four Mathews boys—you brought them up in the same way. Without one thing to do, with not one care in the world. They raced all over creation, from morning to night. They never came home, except to eat and sleep. They didn't know what the word 'duty' meant."

"Precisely." Uncle Jimmy's square jaw hardened suddenly. His gray eyes flashed. "They didn't know what the word 'duty' meant. Nor what several other words meant, either. 'Industry,' for one, 'patience,' for another, 'stick-to-a-tiveness' for another, and 'satisfaction,' for another. Mother and I meant well—oh, yes, we meant well!

"But we cheated those kids out of their birthright, every

last one of 'em. We never saw to it that one of our children had a job of his own. We never taught one child to take up a piece of work and stand by it and put it through—and triumph in his success. We gave, and gave, and gave. We gave 'em everything on earth but the things that really count. We never gave 'em one inch of obligation, not one hour of effort. We handed it all to them on a silver platter. Heaven forgive us!"

"But they turned out well."

"No thanks to us. That was just the good Lord's mercy. And, too, because they—they woke up. They saw their own failings, and they had the pluck and the wisdom to take a stranglehold on themselves, and discipline themselves, even though Mother and I had failed to do our share. It hasn't been an easy job. But every child has put it through. I'm proud of them, of course, for doing it. But I propose to save this crop that effort. And I propose to save Mother and me some pretty anxious years.

He drew a long breath: a shadow of grim memory crossed his face.

"I've figured, and figured, on this. The upshot of my figuring is, Work is the great solution, the Answer to life, for us grown-ups. Why not for children, too? Oh, we're not turning slave-drivers. But each kid is to have his little plot of ground, and be answerable for what grows on it. Each kid is to have whatever pets and animals he wants—and he'll answer for their welfare, too. And each one will have his own small task about the house. Just enough to teach him that the home is his—because he helps to make it a home. *Now* do you get me?"

"I get you. And I'm for you. A hundred percent."

"Glad to hear it. What's more," then he began to grin, a droll, shamefaced, boyish grin, "I'm going in for chores myself. Look at that!" He turned, gestured toward his own handsome, bulky reflection in the shop-window."

"Why—"

Two hundred pounds, and an ounce or so over!" And be sure that there was no Narcissus-complex in the chill stare he bent on his big florid image. "Yes, you'll see me milkin' the cow, and hoeing corn with the best of 'em. I'm going to sweat off a little of this pudge, or die doing it. And Mother—Mother is keener for it than I am. Not that I think there could ever be too much of Mother, but she is getting a bit puffy on hills. And she thinks a course of chores will do her more good than a beauty-parlor."

"It sounds to me as if you'd made the discovery of the ages," said I. "Funny you didn't stumble on it earlier. With either the first, or the second set of children."

Uncle Jimmy gave me his beaming grin at that.

"Third time's the charm," said he.

APPLE BLOSSOMS

AUTHOR UNKNOWN

The townspeople took her at her word—and left her totally alone. Even the children considered her to be an ogre. No one other than those paid to serve her ever spoke to her.

But one . . . someone—a very small someone—dared.

Mrs. Merrill sat on the steps of her big veranda. Shading her eyes with her hand, she gazed down the road. A flock of sheep went by; a lone pedestrian hurried along; several cars hummed past, and all was still, save for the calls of the birds and the humming of a fat bumblebee nearby. The well-kept lawn, dotted with the attractive shrubs and flowers, stretched away down the slope. The house was a huge frame structure of colonial style. It had just received a fresh coat of paint, and the glistening white contrasted sharply with the bright green shutters.

But Mrs. Merrill sighed, as she idly fingered the piece of embroidery work lying on her lap. From out the kitchen window, fragments of song were floating:

> *Ah looked over Jordan, and what did Ah see,*
> *Comin' fo to carry me home,*
> *A band of bright angels comin' after me,*
> *Comin' fo to carry me home.*

Mrs. Merrill bit her lip in vexation. Everything annoyed her. Why couldn't Nina work without singing? She'd spoken to her about it a number of times, but Nina refused to be cowed. "I'll try, Ma'am, I'll try, but it won't do any good. That song is inside of me, and demands to be sung. Besides, if I don't sing it, the fire won't burn, the biscuits won't rise, and nothing will go right."

So, after a few more similarly ill-fated attempts to hush the

singer, Mrs. Merrill gave up. She dared not alienate Nina further, for she was too indispensable. After all, if Nina and her
staff left her, she'd be left totally alone. For she had not made
any acquaintance in the little town at the foot of the hill. Three
years ago she'd come to live in this stately residence, which she
had purchased through her lawyer. From the beginning she'd
made it clear to the people of Bradville that she did not wish
to associate with them. All efforts of the people toward friend-
liness or neighborliness were promptly repulsed. She wanted to
be left alone. Her desire was granted to a degree which should
have satisfied the most exacting person. All attention from the
townspeople ceased; they went about their pursuit of pleasure
or business in much the same way as they had when the great
house on the hill had stood empty and silent. It had become a
foreign thought to them that they should share either their
joys or sorrows with the lady on the hill. Weddings and funer-
als were plenty, but she was neither there to congratulate the
bridal pair nor to drop a tear of sympathy for the mourners.
Bradville was confronted with its problems too, but Mrs.
Merrill had no part in the solution of them.

She seldom left her premises, and when she did, it was to
ride in a luxurious limousine behind drawn blinds. Her chauf-
feur had charge of the minor business affairs which were trans-
acted in Bradville. This left Mrs. Merrill free to avoid any
personal contact with the little town. It was not long until the
aversion became mutual. When the children passed her place
on their way to school, they scampered along and often called
to each other: "Hurry up, or old Lady Merrill will get you!"
Even the dogs slunk away, as though they, too, realized it was
forbidden ground.

Mrs. Merrill had found the isolation she had sought, but somehow it was not as gratifying to her as she had expected. Today she sat in a listless manner gazing at the misty haze that hung over the little valley below.

Swing low, sweet chariot,
Comin' fo to carry me home.

Again the plaintive tones of old Nina broke the silence. Mrs. Merrill impatiently jerked the needle through her embroidery; and moved to a remote corner of the veranda. She was decidedly out of tune with the sentiment of the song. This life was unbearable enough without thinking about the hereafter:

Comin' fo to carry me home.

The faint echo of the song had scarcely died away when the gate clicked. Thinking that it might be Jasper bringing some mail, Mrs. Merrill went to the veranda steps and glanced down the walk. But it was not Jasper's somber face which met her gaze. Just inside the gate stood a little girl about ten years of age. She wore a dress of blue print, which seemed to deepen the blue of her violet eyes. A profusion of dark curls hung about her shoulders, framing a face of unusual beauty. Her slender arms were clasping a great bunch of apple blossoms. She tossed back an unruly curl and smiled up into Mrs. Merrill's face.

"I'm Patricia Ann. Please, may I come in and call on you?"

For a moment Mrs. Merrill was too astonished to speak,

then sharp words sprang to her lips. "Nonsense, child! Go along about your business."

But Patricia Ann did not seem disturbed in the least. "Yes'm," she said sweetly, "that's what I'm doing. At least, I'm going about my daddy's business."

Patricia Ann slowly advanced up the walk until she stood in front of the veranda steps. "It's true, though," she said with a serious nod. "You see, my daddy's the new minister, and it's his business to call on people. We've been here only three weeks, and he's had to work so hard to fix up the parsonage that he hasn't had time to call on many people, so I decided to help him."

"Humph," sniffed Mrs. Merrill. "I don't care for callers."

"That's what I heard," frankly announced Patricia Ann, "but we can't believe everything we hear, you know." The last was stated in a slightly grown-up tone. A hint of a smile appeared on Mrs. Merrill's face for a brief instant. Patricia Ann continued to speak a little hurriedly.

"I wanted so much to bring you some flowers, but there wasn't a thing left—only apple blossoms, so I brought these." She held out the armful of fragrant blooms.

Mrs. Merrill drew a quick little breath. "Oh-h!" The sight and fragrance of the apple blossoms brought a quick rush of memories. Scarcely realizing what she was doing, she reached for the flowers and buried her face in them. After a moment she sat down on the steps and seemed lost in reverie. The little girl perched herself on a lower step and patiently waited. She sent occasional glances toward the lady, who seemed quite unconscious of her presence. Patricia Ann noted the delicately molded white hands that fondled the flowers, the slim throat, the pretty brown tresses, splashed here and there with gray, and most of all, the great dark eyes that at this moment looked so sad and wistful.

"Why you're not very old, at all, are you?" exclaimed the little girl, suddenly breaking the silence.

"What did you say?" asked Mrs. Merrill, coming out of her reverie and resuming her haughty expression.

"I just said that you weren't very old. I thought you were an *old* lady."

"Oh, did you—and what made you think that?"

Patricia Ann's face flushed slightly as she remembered her reason for such a thought. "Old Lady Merrill" was the expression she had heard ever since coming to Bradville, but she instinctively felt that it would never do to mention such a thing. "Well, I just got that idea, I guess," she replied with an embarrassed laugh, and hurried to change the subject. "I don't know many people here, at all. We've been here such a short time, and I've had to look after Larry so Mother and Daddy could fix up the parsonage and make it fit to live in. Daddy said it was in a most—most—" Here Patricia Ann wrinkled her brows in an effort to recall her father's words. "Oh, I know, he said it was in a 'most lamentable condition.' I don't quite know what that means. Perhaps you do."

Again Mrs. Merrill seemed on the verge of smiling. "No doubt," she answered dryly. "What's the matter with the parsonage?"

"Oh, everything—just about. The roof leaks in places, and some of the plaster is off, and the wall paper is hanging by corners. The knobs are most all off the doors, and the floors need paint, and the porch steps are broken, and the gate is off its hinges—and lots of other things that I can't think of now," answered Patricia Ann, finishing with a sigh.

"A nice sort of people to ask a minister to come to live in such a place!" indignantly exclaimed Mrs. Merrill.

"Well, it wasn't all the people's fault," defended Patricia Ann. "We came before they expected us, so things weren't ready."

"Huh! They could have done better than that if they had tried hard enough," retorted the lady with a curl on her lips.

"Yes, I suppose so," agreed Patricia Ann, resting her curly head on the palm of her hand. "We could all do better if we tried harder, you know."

Mrs. Merrill shot a quick, searching glance at the little girl beside her. Patricia Ann was innocently gazing at a fat robin that hopped about on the lawn, so the lady concluded that the rebuke was unintended.

"I don't suppose your father and mother were very happy about coming to such a place, were they?"

"Well, no," acknowledged Patricia Ann. "I don't think Daddy enjoys it, but he's sure God sent him here for some purpose, and he's going to do his very best."

Upon this the lady made no comment. Whatever her thoughts were about the matter, she kept them to herself.

Patricia Ann arose and brushed the folds out of her blue print dress. "I really must be going," she said. "The sun is getting low. I hope you'll let me come again, sometime. It's beautiful up here." The child's eyes quickly swept over the terraced lawn with its gorgeous covered veranda and finally rested on Mrs. Merrill's face with an inquiring glance.

Of course not! The words were on the tip of Mrs. Merrill's tongue, but she forced them back. After all, she'd spent a very pleasant afternoon, and Patricia Ann interested her. It was really no one's business if she wished to amuse herself with this child. "Yes, I think you may," she said, hesitatingly, as though the words cost her an effort. "But mind, you're not to bring anyone else." The last was added in a severe tone.

"No, I won't. I'll just come by myself." Patricia Ann was skipping down the walk. The gate clicked and she was gone. The woman on the steps buried her face in the apple blossoms. When she raised her head, several bright tears glistened on her lashes.

As the summer days wore away, Patricia Ann became a frequent visitor at the big, white house on the hill. Although Mrs. Merrill took the attitude that she was bestowing a favor upon Patricia Ann, in reality these visits had become to her a little oasis in the desert of her loneliness. Patricia Ann would come dancing up the walk in a stiffly starched pinafore, her curls all brushed and shining. She was always full of bits of interesting news about the town, and the problems and trials of the parish. Her sage remarks greatly amused Mrs. Merrill and brought many a smile to that lady's face, in spite of her efforts to keep her composure.

"Mother says we've eaten Daddy's new suit all up," announced Patricia Ann one day as they sat on a rustic bench in the grape arbor.

Mrs. Merrill was taking some very painstaking stitches in her embroidery, so did not answer for a moment. Then she looked up with an odd expression on her face: "Really, now, that's beyond me. How could anyone eat a suit?"

"We did, though." The little girl's face was very sober and a faint sigh escaped from her. "When we came here, Daddy had enough money to buy a new suit, and now we've eaten it all up. Mother feels very bad about it, but Daddy says he'll manage some way. We have to make ends meet, you know."

"Hmm, I suppose. But what's the matter with the people that they can't pay their minister enough to live on?"

"Well," answered Patricia Ann reflectively, "one reason is that they all get such small wages and have such big families. That doesn't work very well." She was loyal in her defense of the parishioners. "I guess the people do the best they can—that is, my Daddy thinks so!"

"Does your father still think that the Lord sent him here for some purpose?" inquired Mrs. Merrill in a tone of amusement.

"Oh, my yes," exclaimed Patricia Ann. "He's very sure about that. 'All things work together for good' you know—for Christians, I mean." As the little girl spoke, she glanced up at the woman's face. What she saw there startled her. Child though she was she could not fail to read the skepticism and unbelief written there. "Why, Mrs. Merrill, aren't you a Christian?" she cried.

A dull red flushed the woman's face, and she drew herself up in her old haughty manner. "Certainly not!"

A deep silence followed, then Patricia Ann spoke very softly. "That's too bad; I'm sorry." And looking into the artless face of the child, the woman could not find it in her heart to resent the remark.

It had become customary for Patricia Ann to visit Mrs. Merrill on Wednesdays and Fridays, but sometimes the duties at home interfered with these visits. "I have to take care of

Larry. Mother's very busy, so I can't come Friday." Mrs. Merrill looked the disappointment she did not express. "Unless I could bring him along. He's such a little fellow, you wouldn't mind having him, would you?"

Mrs. Merrill was very unwilling to lose Patricia Ann's visit, so she finally agreed to the arrangement, although she had some misgivings about having a fussy baby around. However, her fears were promptly forgotten when Patricia Ann came up the walk pushing a little go-cart. The baby wore a blue gingham romper, his head was a mass of golden curls, his cheeks were pink and dimpled. The big, dark eyes danced as he uttered little squeals of delight at every new thing that came into view.

Patricia Ann stopped in front of Mrs. Merrill. Larry looked up at that lady and smiled, as only a baby can smile. He stretched his chubby arms toward her and uttered an unintelligible sound. "Why, he wants you!" exclaimed Patricia Ann. "Why, the idea! He never likes strangers!"

Mrs. Merrill did not say a word, but she fairly snatched the little fellow from his cart and held him close in her arms. In a moment the tears were running down her cheeks and dropping onto the blue romper.

Patricia Ann sat in sympathetic silence. Her quick intuition and habitual association with older people had taught her that there is a time to keep silent. But a question was forming itself in the little girl's mind, which she found hard to repress, so presently she spoke: "Mrs. Merrill, did you—was there ever a baby at your house?"

Mrs. Merrill was hurriedly brushing away her tears as though she were ashamed of them. She nodded in reply to

Patricia Ann's question. "Yes, a baby just like Larry." That was all she said, and Patricia Ann wondered what had happened to him.

"Did he die, Mrs. Merrill?" Patricia Ann's voice was very low. The lady shook her head, but volunteered no further information. Patricia Ann still wondered, but she said no more until the sun began to drop in the west and she realized it was time to go home. Then she made one more attempt to solve the question that was revolving in her mind.

"Well, Mrs. Merrill, if your little boy didn't die, where is he now?"

"I don't know, Patricia Ann." Mrs. Merrill's voice sounded so strange that Patricia Ann glanced up quickly to see if it were really she who was speaking.

"You don't *know*!" the little girl's tone was incredulous. She sat down on the rustic seat and stared at the woman before her.

"That's exactly right, Patricia Ann. I don't know. I sent him away and told him never to come back, and now I don't know where he is." The woman's voice dropped to a despairing whisper.

"Why, Mrs. Merrill, how *could* you?" cried Patricia Ann in astonishment.

The woman paid no attention to the child's outburst but went on hurriedly. "He was all I had; his father died when he was four years old. We had money—lots of it. I gave him everything—everything he wished for until he was nineteen years of age. He had never displeased me in anything. My slightest wish was law. But one night he came home and said he'd been someplace, I don't remember where, and had gotten what he called 'converted.' He ceased to have any interest in our social affairs, and wouldn't even accompany me to the theater, though I pleaded with him to do so. I had great plans and ambitions for his future, but he ignored them all—absolutely refused to do what I wanted him to do. He imagined that God was leading him, just like your father does."

"Oh, but Daddy doesn't imagine it. He *knows* it," corrected Patricia Ann very earnestly.

Mrs. Merrill ignored the correction. "I've been a proud woman, Patricia Ann, a very proud woman." Patricia Ann nodded. That was easy for her to believe. "When my son refused to do the things that I wanted him to do, and began to associate with people who were beneath him, it was too much for my pride. I told him to leave me at once and never return, that I wished never to look on his face again, nor hear a word from him."

Mrs. Merrill paused, and Patricia Ann asked in a sorrowful tone, "And so he *went?*"

"Yes, he went. There was nothing else for him to do. Ah! I was angry, very angry, Patricia Ann, or I would never have said those words."

Patricia Ann saw the pain that looked out of the big, dark eyes of the woman, and she knew that there was bitter repentance there. "You're sorry now, aren't you, Mrs. Merrill?"

The woman gave a little laugh that was a half sob. "Sorry!" she exclaimed. "It seems to me that I've been sorry for a million years!"

"Then why don't you ask him to come back again?"

Mrs. Merrill gave a despairing gesture. "I don't know where he is. It seems as though the great wide world has swallowed him up. I can't find him."

"Well, perhaps he'll come home again, sometime," comforted Patricia Ann.

Mrs. Merrill shook her head. "That's impossible too. I sold our home after he left. I have lived in many places since then. He couldn't find me if he wanted to." The lady arose and picked up her sewing. "Come, Patricia Ann, the sun is almost down. You must hurry." She took a shawl from the seat and tucked it around the baby. "It might be chilly before you get home," she explained. Brushing back his golden curls, she planted a kiss on his soft cheek. "Good night, Patricia Ann. Please don't tell anyone what I told you today."

"All right, Mrs. Merrill, I won't," replied the little girl as she went down the walk, feeling very important with her secret. At the same time, the matter weighed heavily on her heart, and she wished there were some way to bring Mrs. Merrill's boy back to her again. She pondered over the matter a great deal, and grew so quiet at times that it was very noticeable.

"A penny for your thoughts, Puss," said her father one day when she'd been quiet for an unusually long time.

"I can't tell you, Daddy, but I'm thinking about something awfully important."

"I dare say," laughed her father, giving her cheek a little pinch.

A great change had gradually come over Mrs. Merrill. Her haughty expression was gone. Her defiant attitude had changed to one of plaintive resignation. One day when she was sitting idly on the veranda, Patricia Ann flew up the steps, with bright eyes and fly-away curls.

"Oh, Mrs. Merrill, I know what we will do. We'll ask God to find him! I never thought of it before. God helps me find lots of things that I lose. He can find people, too. You see, He knows right where your boy is. He's looking at him right now."

The little girl was quite out of breath, so she dropped to a seat on one of the steps.

Mrs. Merrill gave her an amused smile, yet there was a touch of wistfulness about it. "All right, Patricia Ann, you do that," she said in the tone of one indulging a child in a whim.

Patricia Ann sensed this, for she spoke again more earnestly. "But really, Mrs. Merrill, God promised to answer our prayers. Don't you think He would keep His promise?"

Mrs. Merrill made no reply. The little girl came over and laid her small hand upon the woman's arm. "Mrs. Merrill, if God will bring your boy back to you, will you be a really, truly Christian?"

Tears started in the woman's eyes. "Yes, Patricia Ann," she said brokenly. "Yes, if God will give my boy back to me, I'll be a Christian." She said the last words hesitatingly, as though she were weighing them.

"Well, then, He'll do it, I'm sure," cried Patricia Ann, happily considering the matter settled. In a moment she was skipping over the lawn after a brown and yellow butterfly.

Patricia Ann had soon learned that Larry was even a more welcome visitor than herself. Mrs. Merrill was constantly making excuses for her to bring the boy along. "If it's a nice day, the sunshine will do him good," or "I'm sure your mother is busy and it will be a great help to her," were among her thoughtful suggestions. Patricia Ann seldom came without the curly-headed little fellow, but so many trips were rather hard on the old cart, and it began to go to pieces here and there. One day Patricia Ann appeared, carrying the chubby infant in her arms.

"My, but he's heavy!" she said, panting for breath, as she deposited her burden on the veranda steps. She brushed back the damp curls from her flushed face. "It wouldn't be so bad if he'd just stay inside his clothes, but he's so slippery, he just about gets out of them."

Mrs. Merrill threw back her head and laughed. "Give him to me," she said, and began to pull the baby's garments together in places where they had become sadly separated.

Old Nina heard the laugh that echoed through the veranda. She stopped her work in sudden surprise. She had never heard her mistress laugh like that. "The Lord bless those children," she said, a broad smile on her face. "Thanks to them, a miracle has taken place."

"The cart's broken," briefly stated Patricia Ann, in answer to Mrs. Merrill's question as to why she'd carried the baby. "It's beyond repair, Daddy says, and he hasn't the money to buy another one."

"Isn't your daddy about ready to give up in discouragement over the situation here?"

"Oh, no, I don't think so. I heard him say his favorite verse to Mother this morning."

"What's that?" asked Mrs. Merrill curiously.

Patricia Ann struck a somewhat dignified pose and recited fervently:

> God's purposes will ripen fast,
> Unfolding every hour;
> The bud may have a bitter taste,
> But sweet will be the flower.

Mrs. Merrill felt the hot tears gushing to her eyes, although she could not tell why. She hid her face on Larry's curly head and hurriedly changed the subject.

When the time drew near for the children to go home, Patricia Ann spoke in a troubled voice. "I think this is the last time I can bring Larry, Mrs. Merrill. He's too heavy to carry so far."

"Of course, he is much too heavy for you to carry. He must have a new cart," said the lady decidedly. . . . "Let me see," mused Mrs. Merrill. "You said Larry has a birthday in a couple of months, didn't you?" The little girl nodded, giving him a loving squeeze. "Then I shall give him his birthday present at once, and it will be a new cart."

Patricia Ann received this news with starry eyes. "There's a lovely one at Perkin's store. I saw it the other day."

"What was the price on it? Do you remember?"

"I remember exactly," said the little girl. "It was four dollars." As she spoke, she glanced anxiously at Mrs. Merrill. What if her friend couldn't spare that much money? But that lady gave her a reassuring smile.

"Very well, Patricia Ann, I'll give you the money and you may do the buying. Come inside while I get the money for you."

On one other occasion, Patricia Ann had been in the living room of the big, white house. Its magnificent furnishings had charmed her completely. Today she was much too excited over the new cart to pay much attention to her surroundings. Larry was dumped unceremoniously in the middle of the big rug, while Mrs. Merrill was taking some bills out of a desk in the corner.

"How much did you say it was, Patricia Ann?"

"Four dollars."

"All right, now, here it is. You had better hold it tight." She was holding the bills out to Patricia Ann, but there was no response from the little girl. The woman glanced up wonderingly. Patricia Ann's gaze was riveted on a picture which hung on the opposite wall. It was a large portrait of a young man, standing by an apple tree that was in full bloom. His hands were filled with some of the blossoms. Surprise, wonder, and delight mingled on the face of the child.

"Why, Mrs. Merrill, how—where did you get a picture of my daddy?"

The bills Mrs. Merrill held in her hand fell to the floor unnoticed. "What are you talking about, Patricia Ann? That isn't your daddy!" She said the words sharply.

Patricia Ann chuckled. "As if I didn't know my own daddy!" Again she chucked. "That's just the way he combs his hair now—and there's that dimple in his chin, and—" Here the trembling tone of Mrs. Merrill interrupted her.

"Patricia Ann, what is your father's name?" It had never occurred to her before to ask. She'd been far more interested in the minister's children than in the minister himself.

"My Daddy's name? Don't you know my Daddy's name?" The little girl was still gazing at the picture. "His name is Rev. Joseph Parker. How did you happen to get a picture of him, if you didn't know—" A piercing scream. Mrs. Merrill lay in a crumpled heap upon the rug, white and still.

Old Nina came hurrying in from the kitchen, fearing the worst. "What happened! What happened!" she cried.

Just then the figure on the rug moved slightly and moaned.

"Maybe she's just fainted, Nina," announced Patricia Ann. "Let's put her on the couch."

Nina placed the slender form of her employer on a low

couch, and hurried to the bathroom for the smelling salts and cold water. By the time she returned, the lady had opened her eyes.

"Oh, Mrs. Merrill," said the concerned Nina. "I'm afraid the heat was too much for you. Shall I call the doctor?"

A slight smile passed over the face of her mistress. "No," she said faintly, "call the minister."

"Do you hear *that*, Trisha Ann?" said Nina. " She wants the minister! She must be going to die! Hurry, child, and bring your father!"

Patricia Ann sped down the steps, and away toward town. The baby Larry sat on the living room rug, amusing himself by playing with a costly vase, and pulling the fringes out of a silk scarf on a table nearby.

By the time Patricia Ann had returned with her father, Mrs. Merrill had recovered sufficiently to come into the living room. Two red spots burned in her cheeks, and her eyes were strangely bright.

"Come right this way, Daddy. She's in here," Patricia Ann instructed, as she led her father in toward the living room. "Oh, there she is! Are you better, Mrs. Merrill? Here's my daddy."

But her words fell on deaf ears. Neither the minister nor the woman he had come to visit were aware that she'd spoken. As the young man paused on the threshold of the door, a great light leaped into his eyes, his arms went out in a sudden gesture, he gave a little gasp, and one word fell from his lips: "Mother!" But in that brief gesture, and one word, was the longing of years. In another moment, the woman was sobbing in his arms.

It would be difficult to picture the effect upon Bradville when the news spread around that the lady in the big house on the hill was Mrs. Merrill Parker, the mother of their new minister. It seemed to take the little town some time to recover from the shock, but when it did the reaction was most gratifying. Aversion and ill will changed to sympathy and compassion, as they learned of the long estrangement and the grief of the lonely woman. "I allus said," remarked the blacksmith, "that when people act so strange, they has their reasons. There's allus some reason if it could be found out." People began flocking to church out of curiosity, and many became regular attendants.

Patricia Ann was overjoyed at the astonishing revelation of their kinship to the lady on the hill. It seemed too good to be true. "Grandma," she said one day, "do you remember about that verse that Daddy says, 'The bud may have a bitter taste, but sweet will be the flower?'" Her grandmother nodded. "It has come true, hasn't it, Grandma?" We sure can see now God's purpose in having Daddy come to Bradville. He wanted to answer the prayers about finding your boy. You see, His promises are true."

By this time her grandmother was weeping. "You're right, Patricia Ann. I know you're right. I'll keep my promise to God, too."

The minister and his family were given a pressing invitation to come and live in the big, white house on the hill, but it was graciously declined. "No, Mother, we'd better stay at the parsonage. I think we can minister to the people better from there. They might feel a little strange toward us if we move up with aristocracy." The last was said in a half-teasing, half-serious tone.

"Well, the church surely can't object to having a new parsonage," rejoined his mother. "I'll have them begin right away, and you shall stay with me until it is finished."

"Splendid!" answered the young man. "They've needed that here for years."

"Well, it's time I was making up to Bradville something of what I've withheld from it for so long—and to you, Joseph." She brought out several bank books, and laid them on his knee. "Here is your estate, my son. I've never touched a penny of it."

The minister's face fairly glowed. "Thank God," he said. "I believe that I've had enough experience to use it wisely—for the Lord."

"It's yours. You may do what you like with it," said the contrite woman.

"Grandma, oh, Grandma, where are you?" It was Patricia Ann's voice. She sailed in with a little book in her hand. "I want to read you our memory verse for tomorrow. 'He that winneth souls is wise.' I don't think I quite understand it, though."

"You may not understand the theory, but you surely know how to put it into practice," answered her grandmother meaningfully. And Patricia Ann vaguely wondered why they all smiled.

"Well, I'm not sure I know what it means, but I think it's nice anyway."

Grandmother reached over and drew the little girl close. "I do, too," she whispered. "It makes me think of Patricia Ann and apple blossoms."

THE STEPMOTHER

MARGARET WEYMOUTH JACKSON

How terribly difficult it is to step into some else's mothering shoes. Hilltown High star athlete Arthur (Stretch) Steele knew that, yet he just could not help feeling ashamed of his stepmother's looks, dress, and mannerisms. If only she didn't have to come to the big basketball banquet!

But . . . before the evening was over, Arthur had learned something about both his stepmother and himself that would profoundly change the rest of his life.

The state basketball tournament was over, and a big high school in the northern part of the state had won the championship. And now, over the state, in the cities, and in towns, and in the consolidated high schools, the annual basketball banquets were being held. Nothing but graduation itself exceeded the importance of the basketball banquet, where the players got their letters and the sportsmanship award was made.

Hilltown High had had an unusually good season, and the whole community was fighting for tickets to the banquet. There had never been a Hilltown team that had gone as far in the state tourney as this year's. Everyone knew why they had done so well. Arthur (Stretch) Steele had done it for them. Everyone knew that at the banquet Arthur would get the sportsmanship award, and there was not a boy on the team who begrudged it to him. Everyone knew that the great coach, Mr. Barnes from Central College, who was coming to the banquet as a guest speaker, was coming to ask Stretch about going to Central. Everyone knew it was *his* banquet, right in his hand. And everyone was happy about it—except Arthur himself. He was so miserable that he went about thinking of dire things that might happen to prevent his attending. Since he was usually a quiet boy, self-contained as only a farm boy can be, no one noticed it or knew of his disquiet.

Perhaps his father guessed a little, as the family rode into town together the Saturday before the banquet. Arthur drove, his father sat beside him, and in the back seat the two little sisters sat with his stepmother, holding close to her, talking to her constantly, as they always did. They were going to town to buy a new suit for Mr. Steele and a jacket for Arthur. Mr. Steele looked at his son a little anxiously, but if he knew the boy was not himself, he didn't know why.

"But, Arthur," his father said, in the clothing store, "this suit is sixty dollars! I never paid as much for a suit in my life. It costs more than the suit we ordered for your graduation." He was puzzled and disturbed.

"Of course, Pop," Arthur told him. "It *should* cost more than mine! You take it now. You've got the money—look what you got for your corn!"

"But, if you are going to Central in the fall—"

"Never mind that. You haven't had a new suit all through the war, and it's time you got one."

"Arthur is right," said his stepmother. "You should buy it, David."

Ruth and Daisy stood on either side of her, leaning against her, watching with big eyes.

"If you will buy the hat you liked—the one with the rose on it—then I'll buy the suit!" Mr. Steele spoke to his wife in a voice at once gay and challenging. Arthur did not look at his stepmother, but he was cruelly conscious of her, of her size, her appearance. She was very tall, taller than his father, and she was broad too, for her shoulders were big, her arms were long, and her hands large. She was not fat—simply large. Her face was plain and overlong. *Like a horse's,* the boy thought. She had large brown eyes and a wide mouth. She was not really a homely woman. She was just big and awkward. And with all this she affected things like the hat with the rose on it. She always curled her hair and wore it quite fussy, with little curls across the back of her head. She liked flowered dresses with bright gilt buckles and whole bouquets of silk roses on the shoulders. And the hat! That awful hat she put on, and turned her head to look in the mirror, as unself-conscious as a child.

The boy's heart ached with a dumb love for his father and his father's kindness. He knew his father would never have the heart to tell her how she looked in that hat. He must surely see how she looked! But he concealed it. Well, Arthur would conceal his feelings too. *He could stand it if his father could stand it,* he thought grimly.

He did not know quite when it was that he had begun to notice how other fellows' mothers looked. It was since he had stayed in town so much with his friend Roll March. Roll's mother was slender, and she wore tailored suits and little felt hats. And the minister's wife, Pud's mother, always wore wool dresses and boxy coats, and she generally had a bright red scarf, and her hair in a thick braid on top of her head. And the coach's wife, who was small and dark-eyed and very pretty—he wasn't sure what she wore, but she always looked nice.

Arthur was proud of his father, who was a farmer and made no bones about it. He was brown and clean and neat in his clothes and had a simple dignity that the boy respected profoundly, over and above his unbounded love.

But when Arthur thought of Mr. Barnes, when he thought of the banquet, then all he could see was his stepmother, all dressed up. There would be no one there as dressed up as she would be. He broke out in a cold sweat.

His feelings were complicated. For many years the picture of his own mother had stood on his dresser. He had hung his neckties on it. He had propped other snapshots against it and overlaid it with pictures and programs. Once he had even used it for a frame to dry a snakeskin. But now suddenly he was aware of it. He looked at the picture of his mother every day now. He could remember her quite well, for he had been seven when she died. She was small, with soft dark hair and pretty dark eyes and a sweet smile. She was, he remembered, slender and delicate. She had not survived her thirtieth birthday but had died and left them, the little girls just one and two years old. His stepmother, Agnes, would live to be a hundred. She never even had a cold.

Arthur could remember his mother, and he could remember her death, and the terrible two years that followed, with his father and the baby girls and himself there on the farm, and the odds and ends of women and relatives who had come to "do" for them. Then his father brought Agnes home. She had been kind to them—never in the world had anyone ever been kinder. The boy knew it. She had brought order and peace and security with her. Good meals and clean clothes and comfort. They all loved her. He had never thought, then, about how she looked. His little sisters called her Mother, but he had always called her Agnes as his father did, and she never asked for anything else from him.

So now he was a snob, and he was ashamed of her!

His father was taking the two little girls down to look at the baby chicks at the hatchery.

"Come on, Agnes, I'll buy you a soda," Arthur said.

He took her to the drugstore. He treated her with special courtesy. He smiled at her and teased her. She looked at him with pride, a tall, clean, well-favored boy with darkly blue eyes.

But he could not return her admiration. He could not rise to his own bait. If she would just admit she was a big, clumsy woman and not try to be anything else, there would at least be dignity to her. But she tried so hard to be feminine. She had a little odd way of bending her head—almost coy. The boy groaned. He would soon be off to college. He would never let her know.

His father brought the girls to the store, and at once Ruth and Daisy were telling their stepmother about the chickens. She listened, her eyes as bright as theirs. Some high-school girls came in, flocked around Arthur and his family.

"Oh, Mrs. Steele, you ought to see the decorations we are putting up for the banquet. The gym will look wonderful. We got the big gilded basketball all painted up again, and the place cards are really going to be cute. The art class is making them. Mr. Barnes will be here, and his wife will be with him!"

"I can hardly wait," said Mrs. Steele happily. "It will be wonderful, I know."

"We made out the table chart, and Arthur is to be at the speaker's table. You know what that means!"

Mrs. Steele beamed with pride. The rose in her hat nodded absurdly. She touched Arthur's hand almost shyly, and he gripped hers in a sudden sense of shame at his thoughts.

But he still wished it could be his own mother, so slender and delicate and pretty, at the banquet. He still wished she could have lived, to be with him, to share his honors now. He wished he could introduce Mr. Barnes to his own mother. He wished his father did not have to pretend that he liked the hat with the rose, liked the fussy dresses; that his father was not so enslaved by gratitude for all Agnes had done for them that he had to pretend to like these things.

But Arthur was high-point man and captain of the team, and he had held Donaldson to eleven points—the lowest score the great pivot had made all year. He was the best player on a team that had gone through the season practically undefeated. The whole business of the banquet was his, and he meant to enjoy it! His father and stepmother would be there, earlier than anyone else most likely, and they would get seats close to the speaker's table. Arthur wondered now if the girls were laughing at Agnes. They were laughing at something! Probably at her hat. He hated them.

They got home in time to milk and feed. His stepmother put on a ruffled apron over her print dress and got supper on the table. The girls helped her, setting the table, all of them talking like mad in the kitchen. The time would come, he supposed, when his sisters would feel as he did, when she would look to them as she did to him. Perhaps not. They had known no other mother. They questioned nothing about her. And it was odd, she always dressed them nicely, made all their clothes herself.

His father came in, and they sat down to supper. When David passed his wife's place his hand rested a moment on Agnes' hair, lightly, lovingly. Arthur saw it. He felt only amazement and increased confusion.

The banquet was to be on Monday night. When Arthur went up to bed on Sunday night he found his stepmother in his room. She had pressed his best slacks, had his new sports jacket out, going over the buttons.

"Everything is ready, Arthur. See, I even shined your shoes this afternoon. You'll have to change quickly after school tomorrow. I'll help with the chores so we can all go early. The girls are going to stay with the Reeves. We'll drop them off there."

"You shouldn't do so much for me," he told her. "I'm a big boy now."

She laughed. She always laughed at his little jokes.

"All this winter, whenever you stayed in town, I helped with the chores. You know me. I would rather be out with your father, stringing fence, or working in the garden or helping feed, than to be in the house cooking and cleaning. We always talk about you when we work out together. Your father likes to talk about you. He is so proud of you."

She stopped suddenly as though she had said too much. She stood there in the posture which irked him so—her neck was bent, her head drooped forward—as though to deny her height, her strength. The impulse of kindness which had come to him withered. He did not know what to say to her at all. Then she was gone. Her step was light on the stairs. He wished he had said something to her, thanked her for all she had done for all of them. It was something he must say soon, before he went away to college, and it must be said at some natural time. He felt almost sick with a sense of failure and defeat.

All day Monday, in school, Arthur felt as though he might be coming down with the flu. He was feverish, and his bones ached. Even his teeth hurt, and he had a pain in his chest. The whole high school was in a state of seething excitement over the banquet. Students were excused from classes to set tables. The decoration committee strung maroon and white paper against the tile walls. Boys were setting up the long tables and unfolding the stacked collapsible "funeral" chairs. The domestic-science teacher unrolled white paper for tablecloths. Vases of flowers were set out at intervals. Knives and forks borrowed from church kitchens were added to the high school's supplies.

The boys on the team were not supposed to work, but they stood about, lending a hand, important and full of their own significance.

Roll's mother, Mrs. March, came into the gym in a new spring suit, her dark hair in a smooth roll. She was on a committee. She showed Arthur how the tables were arranged.

"We want your people to sit here," she said, putting down their place cards. "And Mr. Barnes will sit right opposite, over here, with Mr. Hicks on one side and you and the school coach on the other. The girls will stand here to sing. Your mother is getting a little deaf, you know, and we want her to hear everything."

He was thinking of something else. He asked her, "Did you know my own mother?"

"Why, yes, Arthur. Yes, I was in school with her. Why?"

"Oh, I've just been thinking of her. I remember her as so pretty. I just wish she could be here tonight, that's all."

She looked at him a little oddly. "She wasn't much of a hand to go places," she said. "Her health was never good; it did not permit much activity. I don't think she ever went anywhere after Ruth was born."

Maybe she should never have had Ruth and Daisy, he thought, although he simply could not imagine a world without the merry and giggling little sisters in it. But evidently the three of them had been too much for his delicate little mother. Someone else had to raise them! He was jealous for her, for all she had missed.

When he got on the school bus to go home they were already frying chickens in the domestic-science kitchens. The girls who were to wait on the tables would wear maroon and white crepe-paper aprons, and the six who were to sing would step out and stand in a row together. Mr. Hicks, the principal, would tell some good jokes, and the coach would have every man on the team stand up to be applauded. Mr. Barnes would make his talk; then they'd give the big award.

There was just time to get the chores done and hurry to dress. Agnes had everything organized. They got ready quickly and quietly. Arthur could hear his father and Agnes talking in their room. He couldn't hear what she said, but his father spoke loudly.

"Now take your time and fix your curls," his father said. "They'll look pretty under your new hat . . . Yes, I'll wait and button your dress." That meant she was going to wear the pink dress with the blue flowers on it. She had sent away for it. It was too short, and she had lengthened it with a wide hem of blue to match the flowers. And the curls. *And* her big hands and feet and tall strong body . . . What was it Roll's mother had said about her? Something about her hearing. He noticed that his father often lifted his voice when he spoke to her. She seemed so—indestructible. Could it be possible something was the matter with her? He didn't believe it. It was just natural to speak to her in a decided tone.

Arthur drove the car, and when he stopped at the neighbor's he took a little sister by each hand and led them up to the house, giving each of them a friendly swat when he left them.

At the school, he parked the car near the gym among the other cars and went in with his father and his stepmother. Everyone who could get a ticket was there, which meant half the town. He greeted his friends. People were speaking kindly to his father and stepmother. The Methodist minister was telling a funny story and everyone was laughing. Arthur sat with Mr. Barnes and Mr. Hicks and the coach at the head table.

Mr. Barnes was a big and very pleasant man, with steel-bright eyes, a gruff voice, and a wide smile. Arthur liked him at once.

The team sat facing Arthur, and just beyond was his father, who looked very nice in his new suit; his wife sat beside him. Her head was bent a little; the hat with the rose on it was stuck on top of her thick curled hair, and no one else had a dress like hers—no one had anything *remotely* like it. All the other women in the room had on dark dresses or suits, and their heads were either bare or they wore small hats.

Arthur did not eat what was on the plate set before him. He did not hear the girls sing "Sylvia," or notice that Bonny—who led the sextet and who was the prettiest girl in high school and the one he admired most—was flirting with him. He didn't see the bright faces of the waitresses or the faces of his teammates. And then Mr. Barnes was speaking, and a little of what he said filtered through to Arthur.

Mr. Barnes was telling them about how he had grown up in the hills and had started playing basketball out of doors.

"We never had a gym," he said. "We played on an outside court the year round. Once we played a game in a storeroom that still had shelves on the walls, and did we get skinned! My father," he told them, "was a just man, but my mother was one of those people who always knew more about the game than the referees, and she was very partisan. I could hear her voice all over the floor."

Everyone was laughing, and Mr. Barnes spoke of his mother as though she were a terrible old hillbilly—and as though he had loved her better than anyone in the world.

Arthur lost track again. He was looking at his father, who had put his arm across the back of his wife's chair and was leaning toward her as though he could hear better if he were closer to her—or as though to help her hear. A strand of her hair had come loose; his father tucked it back under the silly hat, a gesture rich with a simple, uncomplicated love.

A shiver went over the boy and something happened to him. Why, his father was not just patient and loyal. He *loved* Agnes! He loved her hat, her curls, her bright dress. He loved everything about her.

She was listening to Mr. Barnes, her eyes on his face with a concentrated expression, and Arthur knew suddenly that she *was* getting hard of hearing. He felt an almost violent throb of compassion for her. He thought: She *is* feminine. She is as feminine as she can be. She loves the rose, the curls, the color. And she's right. She'd look a lot worse in plain, severe clothes. She would look like a man. Some dainty, slender woman could wear tweeds and sports clothes. Her instinct was against all that. Her taste, unquestionably, was very bad, but still she had an instinct to adorn herself. And his father loved her!

The way she bent her neck—it was to hear better. And more than that, it was because she was truly modest. Even a little shy. She didn't want to intrude upon him. She probably felt his criticism and was helpless against it. But her long, kind face—he saw now that, although her body was strong and big, her mind was delicate, tender. That was what his father saw. All at once Arthur liked the way she looked. It made her different; it was something he would talk about with tender amusement when he grew old. "You should have seen the clothes my stepmother wore! She was wonderful!"

He loved her!

A great bursting happiness welled in him. He caught her

eye. He winked at her and made a little gesture, making an O with thumb and forefinger. . . . They were giving him the sportsmanship award. They were calling for a speech from him. He got up and stood there, a little giddy. He spoke impulsively, from his heart.

"There's somebody else deserves this more than me," he said. "If she hadn't done my chores, I couldn't have played ball." And he moved quickly around the end of the table and put the small silver cup into his stepmother's hands.

Everyone was cheering and clapping. The banquet was over. Arthur took Agnes' big hands in his own and led her up to Mr. Barnes. "This is my mother," he said with pride.

Mr. Barnes shook hands with Agnes. "I can see where the boy gets his height," he said, "and I want to talk to you people about letting him come up to Central."

Arthur squeezed his stepmother's hands as at a shared joke, and they let it stand that way.

ZACHARY'S ANGEL

RUTH LEES OLSEN

Zachary, a crippled orphan raised by an aunt who detested all boys, lived out days and nights etched in pain. But then he gained possession of the miniature of his mother's lovely face his father had always carried with him, and began carving it into stone.

Thus was born "Zachary's angel."

"Get out of here, you good for nothing, and take your junk with you. The very idea of a boy your size wasting his time whittling pieces of wood, or making mud pies."

The angry voice of the irate woman crashed on the ears of the white-faced cripple like pelting hail on a shorn lamb. Hurriedly he gathered up the clay he had been molding, and the bits of wood he had been carving, and dragged himself off the porch down the weed-grown pathway to the old, unused barn by the millstream, easing himself down in the doorway, where the sunshine, at least, smiled a friendly welcome. The hot tears that welled up in his eyes made rain mists of the sunbeams, but he was used to that, for many, many times before, the unfortunate boy had found in tears his only comfort.

Zachary Fillmore, named after his great-great-grandfather, a veteran of the Civil War, besides being an orphan, which was bad enough in itself, was also a hopeless cripple. When but a baby, he had been dropped by a careless nurse, and the injury then received caused a deformity of the lower part of his body. But his head, well shaped and set on broad shoulders, was topped by a mass of dark, curly hair, and his expressive gray eyes could, on occasion, grow dark with passion or gleam with a friendly sympathy. But he hated his crutches, and sometimes questioned God's wisdom in allowing such a disfigured creature as himself to live.

Things were not quite so bad while his parents had been alive. His mother had given her crippled boy the most loving care, and never had she been too tired or ill to minister to his needs. And Zachary, in turn, had fairly worshiped his "Rosebud mother," as he always called her. His father had never meant so much to him, for try as he might, John Fillmore could not conceal his disappointment in his son. He had always planned that his heir should uphold the dignity of the family name, but he could not go to the world and say, with the Fillmore pride in his voice, "This is my son. Someday he will walk in his father's steps." And Zachary, sensing his father's disappointment, did his best to keep out of his sight.

His father passed away first, and then his mother, and it seemed to the crippled lad that the very light of day had been blotted out in the darkness of his despair, as he realized that he was an orphan.

Miss Amanda Fillmore, his father's only sister, came to care for the house, and incidentally for her nephew. She was a maiden lady of uncertain disposition, and had no love for boys. They were noisy, troublesome nuisances! Now she must take charge of one of these detestable creatures, and he a cripple at that! There was neither love nor pity in her heart for Zachary.

She never stinted him on food or clothes, for ample provision had been made in the will for all of that, and his wants were small in those lines. Also, his allowance of spending money was sufficient for his materials for wood carving and clay molding. She never beat or abused him physically, but there is a torture keener even than the rod. At times Aunt Amanda's tongue seemed dipped in vitriol, and her words lashed and stung as no whip could ever do.

The boy's affliction had made him supersensitive. He felt that he could do nothing to please her, and often he wondered if there was any use in making the effort. She had no patience with the work he loved so dearly. Not only did she make fun of his efforts, but she also destroyed his material if it happened to be in her way.

Zachary loved his carving and modeling. It was the outward expression of a soul that craved beauty, and was the one ray of light that shone through the mists of his affliction. With the soul of a true artist, he admired all nature, seeing beauty even in common clay. Under the manipulation of his skillful fingers, it grew into articles of quaint and rare design.

Mr. Jackson, the man who owned the marble quarry close by, was a friend of Zachary's. They first met during a heavy rainstorm, when the cripple had dragged himself to shelter in the tool house on the edge of the quarry. He was chilled and dripping wet, but his cold fingers still clung to some bits of marble he had found on the road. Mr. Jackson exchanged the shivering lad's wet coat for a dry one of his own, and then, noticing the marble chips, drew from him something of his great love. After that, the quarryman often left pieces of marble at the old barn, and Zachary made good use of them.

While his parents had been alive, the boy had studied under a private tutor, but Aunt Amanda thought this a needless expense, and sent him to the public high school. The first week was torture to the sensitive boy, and as he clumped down the hall after the closing bell on Friday afternoon, he passed a group of his classmates in time to catch the words: "There goes old Clumpy. Wouldn't he be fine to mark time for a regiment of soldiers?" But Zachary showed no resentment. It was useless, he knew, for they were all strong, husky boys, while he was hardly an apology for one. With head bowed and teeth clenched to hold back the tears, he left the building. It was hard enough to endure physical suffering without being held up to ridicule;

so he informed his aunt that he would not return to school. And in spite of her tirades and threats, he held to his purpose. There was a public library nearby, he pointed out, so he need not remain an ignoramus.

Disgusted and disgruntled, Aunt Amanda declared that he was good for nothing, and would be better off dead. Sometimes the misunderstood, discouraged boy wished her words might come true. But the thought of his beloved mother and her faith in him caused him to throw back his shoulders, set his lips firmly, and vow to himself, "Someday she'll be proud of me. I have two good eyes to see beauty with and two good hands to help me capture and reproduce it. I'll show her. Yes, I will!"

Zachary had one unfailing source of comfort. He had found it one day when he was so blue and despondent that he could not even work, and was dragging his crippled limbs down the roadway toward the inviting woods. As he neared the entrance to the Westport Orphans' Home, he saw a wistful-eyed little boy, with freckled face pressed against the iron bars of the big gate. Jimmie was lonesome. He did wish so much that he had somebody he could call his very own, and who would take a special interest in him. In this place he was nobody but just one of the orphans!

The plaintive look in the boy's eyes touched Zachary's heart and made him forget for a moment his own bitterness and troubles.

"Hello. Want to go walking?"

Instantly the longing look turned to joyful anticipation. "Oh, do I want to go walking—" Then a shadow crossed his face. "But we can't go nowhere, 'less the matron says so. Maybe"—more hopefully—"you could ask her."

Zachary dropped down on the greensward outside the orphanage fence with a sigh of relief. The sun was hot, and he was tired, more so than he had realized. "I'll do that very thing someday, and we'll go walking down where the dandelions grow. And we'll gather a great big armful."

Jimmie reached one little brown hand through the iron bars and laid it affectionately on his new friend's shoulder. "Say, that would be fine! I love dandelions. But it's too bad you're crippled. We can't go far."

Zachary winced, and turned his head so the boy might not see the misery in his face. But Jimmie was quick to understand. "I didn't mean it that way. It's better to have crutches an' get out in the sunshine than to stay in an ol' hospital bed for weeks, and weeks, and *weeks*!"

"What do you know about hospitals, sonny?"

"Lots. I had a fever, an' they sent me over to the hospital all by myself. Nobody could see me but the nurse, an' whenever she came she brought nasty ol' medicine. An' she was always so cross, an' scolded terribly when I didn't keep the bedcovers straight. I didn't have a thing in the world to do but play with my fingers. There weren't even any pictures on the walls! An' anyway, I couldn't of seen 'em if there had been, 'cause the nurse kept the blinds pulled down."

"How long were you in quarantine there?" questioned Zachary.

"Most a million years," was the boyish reply. "An' was the sunshine great when I got out!"

Just then Mr. Jackson drove by on his way to the village, and seeing the boys, stopped to talk with them. He listened to Jimmie's plea for a visit with his newly found friend, and since he was one of the directors of the executive board of the Westport Orphans' Home, promised to see if the matter could be arranged. Zachary was glad for a ride back to town with the quarryman, and as he painfully climbed out of the buggy in front of the old red barn, where he had his workshop, his friend took from his pocket several pieces of marble, saying, "My wife and I were pleased with the little horse you carved for us. It's the exact image of old Molly."

Mr. Jackson was as good as his word, and soon Jimmie was allowed to visit his friend once a week. The little boy came to look forward to those time as "heavenly days." He felt now that he really belonged to some one, for Zachary called him "little brother," and that title lifted him above being just an "orphan."

One day he came racing into the old red barn, his face aglow with enthusiasm. "Say, Zachy, I have an idea. Why don't you make an angel—an honest-to-goodness one with wings an' everything?"

Amused at the request, Zachary inquired, "What do you know about angels?"

Jimmie looked a little doubtful. "Not so much. But a lady came to the orphanage last week to talk to us boys, an' she told us that everybody has an angel to take care of him. 'Course, I don't think orphans have angels. There isn't any one to tell God we need 'em. But we do, Zachy, yes, we do. So I've been a-thinkin' that you could make us one out of marble. There's a little place on the stairs where it could sit, an' us boys could see it every night when we go to bed. You'll do it for us, won't you, Zachy?"

But the crippled lad would not promise. He was not acquainted with angels, so was not sure that he could reproduce one in marble. That night he hunted up the old family Bible and slowly turned the pages till he found a picture of angels. His aunt, watching him, remarked that she was "glad he was beginning to think about his soul's salvation," but he did not tell her what he proposed to do. He looked at the picture carefully, and finally decided that he could carve the form of an angel without difficulty, but the faces in the picture looked so stony and hard! He was sure *real* angels did not look like that! What should he do?

The next time Mr. Jackson made a visit to the old red barn, Zachary told him of Jimmie's request, and his problem.

"The face?" he mused thoughtfully. "Well, now, don't you know someone who looks like an angel?"

Instantly Zachary knew whose face should grace his angel. His mother's! Hers was the most beautiful face he had ever seen. His father had carried her miniature wherever he went. It was painted on porcelain and set in a frame of gold. He remembered the picture well, and, furthermore, he knew that it belonged to him. But Aunt Amanda had taken possession of it when she came, and locked it up in his father's desk, till she could be sure he was old enough to appreciate its value. Zachary decided he must secure this picture now. He knew where the keys to his father's desk were kept; so one day when his aunt was out, he slipped into the sitting room and procured the treasure.

After this, the work of the angel went forward rapidly. And as he studied and worked, the crippled boy gradually lost his spirit of bitterness, and a more kindly feeling took its place. Heaven and heavenly things grew nearer and dearer. Mr. Jackson noticed the difference in his attitude toward life, and rejoiced in the change. "It's wonderfully lifelike," he said, praising Zachary's work. "Someday your angel will speak to the heart of everyone who sees it."

At last the statue was finished, but the boy could not bring himself to the point of parting with it. He had learned to love it, and there seemed to be so little that was really his own.

Finally Jimmie brought things to a head one day when both he and Mr. Jackson had stopped at the old red barn for a visit.

"Isn't the angel finished, Zachy?" he pleaded. "Can't I take it home today? The boys say I just *have* to find out when it's coming. You see, I've told them all about it, and they can't wait much longer. Come on, Zachy, let me."

"Sure enough, Zachary," echoed the quarryman, "isn't the angel ready for the boys to see yet?"

Zachary was silent for a moment, then quietly indicating the place they should stand, he slowly removed the cloth that covered the statue. There was a gasp of surprise from Jimmie, who had not seen it for some weeks.

"Why—why—it's a *real* angel!"

Mr. Jackson, even though he had watched the young sculptor at work, hardly expected anything quite so beautiful as the angel before him. "That, my boy," he said quietly, "is a real work of art."

"And to think it's all mine!" cried Jimmie, exultantly, then, as an afterthought, "I mean it belongs to us orphans. Oh, goody, goody! Can we have it today, Zachy?"

Zachary looked beseechingly at his friend, but Mr. Jackson was busy admiring the statue. "I'll see the board of directors right away to arrange a time for presentation, for this angel is worthy of a special program."

After the departure of his friends, Zachary fought the hardest battle of his life. His angel was more to him than a piece of marble. Every stroke of the chisel had brought his mother closer to him, until her memory had become a living, pulsing thing that had brought a peace and happiness such as he had never known. And now he must give it up. He just *could not*. But even as these thoughts raced through his mind, something told him that the law of love is the law of sacrifice, and that the surrender of one's dearest and best is but the promise that someday it will come back again a thousandfold more beautiful. Strengthened and comforted, he took the precious miniature from his breast pocket, where he kept it next his heart, and gazed into his mother's eyes long and lovingly. When he replaced it, the victory was won.

It was on a Monday morning that Mr. Jackson came for the statue. "It's all arranged, Zachary," he said. "The Westport Orphans' Home will welcome your angel with open arms. We are to have a presentation program this afternoon, and I am coming after you."

At first Zachary stubbornly refused even to consider attending the exercises, but when his friend spoke of the bitter disappointment of the boys if he should remain away, he finally consented to go, if he could be seated where he could see and not be seen.

So as the time for the program drew near, the cripple found himself seated in a part of the chapel where he had a full view of the stage, and could also see the boys as they marched in, but where he was himself hidden from view. Zachary wished with all his heart that he had feet that could keep time to the stirring march as the orphans filed down the aisles to their seats. Yes, there was Jimmie, and his face was radiant with joy.

Now the speakers and guests of honor were taking their seats on the platform—the president of the school board, the matron, the directors, Mr. Jackson, a distinguished-looking stranger, evidently a foreigner, and—who could that be but Miss Amanda Fillmore? Zachary felt a sinking sensation in the region of his stomach. Surely as his aunt saw the face of his angel, she would guess that he had taken the miniature. His hand nervously clutched at the bit of porcelain next to his heart.

He scarcely heard the first two or three speakers, so interested was he in watching the orphans, and a feeling of thankfulness filled his heart that he had been permitted to bring this bit of joy to them. Then Mr. Jackson gave the history of the statue, and as he told the story of the crippled boy and his work, more than one person on the platform dabbed furtively with his handkerchief at the suspicious moisture around his eyes. The president accepted the angel in the name of the Westport Orphans' Home, and called upon "our distinguished visitor," M. Angelo Balabo, to say a few words.

Zachary thrilled at the name. So *that* was who the stranger was! He had read much of this famous sculptor, but had never even dared hope to see him. He listened intently as M. Balabo spoke of the value of art to the world. He congratulated the people of Westport on having such a promising young artist as a native son, and predicted that some day he would bring fame to the community. Then he unveiled the statue. There followed a deep hush, then applause that almost rocked the building in its intensity.

The boy-artist from his refuge let his gaze wander from the appreciative audience of orphan boys to the face of his aunt. It indicated, in quick succession, surprise, bewilderment, disfavor, and anger, as she recognized the striking resemblance between the face of the angel and that of her brother's wife. The only likeness of her sister-in-law which she knew of was the porcelain miniature that she had kept locked up in the desk at home.

Zachary sensed that big trouble was in store for him, and resolved to hurry home as soon as the program was over and slip the precious miniature back into its original hiding place before his aunt arrived. But Jimmie and his pals surrounded and detained him. Therefore when he finally clumped slowly across the porch and into the living room, Aunt Amanda was waiting.

"Give me that picture this minute!" she demanded. "Any boy who'll—"

"Wait a minute, Miss Fillmore." Mr. Jackson interrupted her tirade. With him was the visiting sculptor, and together they entered without waiting for an invitation. It was Zachary who offered them chairs, for Miss Amanda seemed unable to collect her scattered wits. Angelo Balabo addressed himself at once to her, for he was a busy man, and had no time to waste. "Your nephew, you call him?" he questioned, indicating the boy. "He will be one grand artist someday. But he needs training. He must have study. And I come to ask, that you let me take him with me. I have no son. He shall be mine. Yes—you will let him go?"

Aunt Amanda gasped in surprise, and started to make excuses. She drew her handkerchief and wiped her eyes. "He is all I have, and I hardly see how I can spare him. Besides, there is all the expense—"

But the artist interrupted her. "No expense. He shall live with me, and in time he will pay me back one hundredfold."

"Is there no money left the boy from his father's estate?" questioned Mr. Jackson.

"Yes," she acknowledged, but it was not a great amount, and she felt that she should be cautious in the use of it, since her nephew had no other near relative and she was responsible for his care.

M. Balabo, however, waved aside every objection, and she finally had to give her grudging consent to the plan.

"Then it is settled, and you will go?" he cried enthusiastically, turning to the boy, who stood by with glorified face and tear-filled eyes. Zachary could only nod his head. But Mr. Jackson, sensing the boy's deep emotion, assured the artist that he was too delighted for words.

That evening, as Mr. Jackson came to say good-bye, for they were leaving in the morning, the boy said, "No one but God knows how I have longed to be a real artist. But I am such an ugly, misshapen piece of humanity, I never thought of having any talent. Oh, I do hope I can make good."

His friend looked at him quizzically. "If you're going to waste time thinking about your looks, you might as well stay right here and develop ugliness. But if you keep in mind the great need of humanity for the beauty and the high ideals you can give them, then you will succeed. You can't change your body, but you can carve out the angel in your own soul, and thus inspire others to attempt great things, no matter what their handicaps."

Zachary's face at that moment reflected the radiant expression he had learned to love in the miniature of his mother. "I can never repay you, Mr. Jackson, for the inspiration you have given me. You saw beauty where there was none, and I, too, will do the same until others learn that disappointment, pain, sorrow, are but tools to be used in carving life's angels."

WHEN THEY ALL CAME HOME

AGNES SLIGH TURNBULL

other was old and had long yearned for all the children to come home. But only once had they come, and that was for Father's funeral. Would it take another one to bring them home?

This is a story that every grown child ought to read at least once a year.

Mother sat at her window and stared out at the lane which led past the cornfield to the public road. In her lap lay six letters which she had just finished reading, and which her thin, wrinkled hands still fumbled gently.

Six letters in one mail was an unprecedented happening. At first, when she had seen Lizzie coming down the lane from the rural mailbox with her hands full of white envelopes, she had felt vaguely alarmed. There must be something the matter with the children! Then, with the letters before her, she remembered. It was the twenty-eighth of September. The large calendar, which displayed its great black numerals along with a highly colored landscape and the name and attributes of the New Salem general store from the wall above the table, confirmed it. She was eighty years old that day.

It was because an eightieth birthday sounded so much older than any of those in the seventies, Mother supposed, that the children had taken note of it and written. Alice would be the one to plan the little surprise, she decided now, as she gazed down the lane. But whether the boys had to be reminded or not, it was good to hear from them. They didn't write very often.

She brought her eyes back again to the letters and their enclosures. Alice and Laura had both sent lace handkerchiefs. These would be added to the already large and unused supply in the upper bureau drawer. The boys had all sent banknotes. She had not even noticed the denomination, but they would all go into the tin box on the mantelpiece. Bank notes are even more useless than lace handkerchiefs, at eighty.

But they were good children. They wanted to be kind to her. She thought of each one as she scanned their letters again. Laura's was full of news of herself and her family: how the children were growing up; how busy she was with them and her many social duties; how well Will was doing in his profession. She enclosed a sample of her new evening dress.

The boys' letters were all much alike in substance: there were five fine lines from Joe, the banker; two pages of large scrawl from Wesley, who ran a newspaper; and one page each from Howard in the state capitol, and from John, who taught in a college.

They wished her a happy birthday; they were well and very busy; their families were all well and very busy (the word "busy" seemed somehow to permeate the pages!); the weather was beginning to seem like fall; they hoped she was well and comfortable. So they all ran.

Alice's was the tenderest of all, and Mother cried a little over it. But in none of them, not even in Alice's, did she find the thing for which her eager old eyes sought through page after page—a hint that one of them was coming soon to see her.

The last visits had been from the girls in June. This was September. Not so long, and yet days of half idleness go so slowly.

The boys took turns in coming each spring for a day. They rather boasted of their punctilious performance of this duty. To Mother, these visits seemed like curious troubled dreams when they were over. For days beforehand she followed Lizzie about the house, nervously trying to help put the already immaculate rooms in a more perfect state of readiness. It was her hand that gave the bed in the "spare room" its final touches: smoothing faint wrinkles out here, tucking the spread a little tighter there, herself lifting the lid of the big blanket box after Lizzie had gone downstairs, and drawing out painstakingly the old silk patchwork quilt which she allowed no one but herself to fold and unfold, to lay on the foot.

The night before the great day she never slept much. How *could* she? Lizzie had insisted upon putting sage in the chicken dressing, and one of the boys, Mother felt sure, did not eat it. Which one was it? She racked her brain to remember.

Then the weather! Henry had not finished painting the covered buggy, and would have to meet the train with the open one. If it should be wet tomorrow! She crept cautiously out of bed to scan the sky again. There were clouds. Her feet were cold when she got back in, and her head ached a little. She must sleep and be ready to enjoy the visit.

But what about Sims? It seemed too bad not to ask him over for supper. He always expected it, having grown up with the boys. As early as February, Sims always began making excuses to discuss the coming visit.

"Guess Howard's about due this year, ain't he? My, I'd like to see Howard! I mind when him an' me used to sit in the back seat together at school." Or perhaps, "I s'pose it's Joe that'll be droppin' in on you this spring? My, I'd give anything to see Joe. Do you remember when him an' me used to run off an' go coon huntin' with old Brownie?"

None of the boys seemed to care much about Sims's society now; but he was her nearest neighbor and unfailingly kind to her. And it pleased him so to come. Invariably, she'd decide to ask him "this once more."

Before six o'clock on the morning of each of these visits, Mother rose unrefreshed, but nervously eager and active. She disclaimed all help in getting into her black silk dress. She tied her white apron with trembling fingers. Then, after a hasty breakfast, put on her 'far-away' glasses and sat down by the window to watch the road. Henry, who ran the farm and did the outside work of the place, had gone to meet the train.

At last a horse's head came in sight around the curve of the cornfield. Mother strained forward and called Lizzie. Lizzie ran to the other window.

"Aw, that's Kennedy's milk wagon. Now, don't you go an' get all excited. They ain't had time to get here yet."

After more endless waiting, a horse's head appeared above the cornfield. Mother restrained herself but sat forward tensely. The horse turned down the lane. A man sat beside Henry in the open buggy. Lizzie had seen them too, and called out, "Here they come."

Mother was at the front door when the buggy stopped. Her heart beat fast. He was here. Her boy, her little boy. She saw him as he used to come, whistling in from the barn—

Then suddenly a stranger sprang out, with Henry following with the traveling bag. A large stranger, grayish of hair and inclined to stoutness, smelling of clean, faint, unusual city odors. He grasped her in his arms:

"Why, Mother, you're looking fine! Not a day older," he said as he kissed her.

For that one minute, as she held him, he was all hers.

Then he turned quickly to shake hands with Lizzie, who had been the "hired girl" while he was still at home, and who now, flushed with embarrassment and pleasure, was trying to shake hands elegantly and at the same time make sure that Henry didn't enter the hall with his muddy boots.

Then there was breakfast for the guest, though he assured them a trifle irritably that he had eaten on the train and wanted nothing more. Mother insisted upon pouring his coffee—and spilled it! Lizzie exclaimed over the spot on the table-cloth. The guest looked bored. Mother slipped away to the pantry and laboriously reached a jar of preserves which she knew Lizzie had forgotten. With her own hands she opened them and poured them into the little blue pickle dish which the children had always loved. She brought them to the table and presented them at his elbow. He waved them lightly aside and went on talking to Henry about the crops.

Mother sat down, hurt, baffled. She began to ply him with questions about himself and his family, anything to have his eyes again upon her. He answered them all, enlarged for a few minutes upon some of them, then, getting his hat, said he believed he would go out and have a look at the farm.

He was gone till noon.

Mother puttered about restlessly and watched the windows. He came in at last buoyantly. The old fields were looking fine. The new orchard was going to be better than the old one. He was hungrier than he'd been for months. Mother beamed, and dinner was almost happy.

When the meal was ended, however, Lizzie was inexorable about the regular afternoon nap. Mother had to yield. She called to him from her bedroom door.

"I'll just take a little cat-nap, and then we can visit. I'll be fresher then, maybe."

"To be sure," he answered. "You take your sleep, and then we'll talk."

She woke at two o'clock, startled. She had slept a whole

hour. She hurried to the sitting-room. The house was very quiet. Lizzie sat sewing in the sunny window.

"Where—where is he?" mother quavered.

"Gone to town," Lizzie returned calmly. "Henry took him. He wanted to look round the old burg, I guess. They'll be back soon."

Mother sat down at her window to watch the lane. She watched for two hours, then at four o'clock they returned. He was faintly apologetic.

"Had no intention of staying away so long. Met some of those old duffers I hadn't seen for years, and couldn't get away from them. Had a good sleep, Mother?"

Sims arrived. There was supper, and a little time afterward in the sitting-room. But she was weary, and forgot what she had wanted to say. The next morning, an early, hasty good-bye, and he was gone. She watched him out of sight, up the lane, and around the cornfield.

So, with slight variations, the annual visits from the boys had gone for years. Before Father's death it had been much the same. In the last years of his feebleness, it had moved her strangely to see him standing by the window, watching, watching them out of sight. She had pitied him more than herself.

Together they had held one great longing: to have the children home once, all together; all around the table as they used to be; all about the fire in the evening; all in their old childhood rooms at night; once again, all together under the old roof with them. In his faltering, nightly prayers, Father had prayed for it; in long conversations at the winter fire, under the summer shade of the pear tree or at night when they both lay sleepless, they had planned for it.

They spoke of it to the children, one by one. Father wrote eager plans in his trembling script for one Thanksgiving, then for a Christmas, then for spring, and then again and again. Each time a dozen valid reasons seemed to keep most of them away. There were always explanations, apologies, and fair promises for "another time."

When the fulfillment came at last, the bitter irony of it cut into Mother's soul. Father had gone suddenly in the night. Lizzie and Henry lived then in the small tenant house and Mother was quite alone. She had telephoned the telegrams to the children herself as soon as she realized what had happened. And by the next night they were all there—for the first time in twenty years, just as she and Father had planned—but with Father not there to see.

Through her dazed grief, Mother puzzled over it. Not one this time had made an excuse. They had come promptly, willingly it seemed, when it mattered very little, except for the curious comments of the neighbors, whether they were all there or not. The boys had even stayed three days and the girls longer, on pretense of making arrangements for her. But there were few to make. With barely visible relief they had agreed to her plan of staying on in the old place, with Lizzie and Henry to move into the big house with her and manage the farm as usual.

That was ten years ago. In that time, Mother had passed from a sturdy activity to a quietly passive old age. Lately she had thought much of the time when she, too, would go. She hoped it would be quickly and quietly in the night, as Father had gone. And she felt no fear. At eighty, one lives as it were with one's bag ready packed for a long and sudden journey. Mother's preparations were all made. The simple, serene faith of a lifetime was with her still; and, in a more literal sense, there lay in the under drawer of the bureau the white garments she would need for the journey. Lizzie knew just where to lay her hand on them quickly.

There was only one thing Mother dreaded. And this dread had increased year by year until it had become a dark, fixed thing in her consciousness. It was the thought that after all the lonely years, lightened only by brief glimpses of her children, as they came hurriedly, one by one, there should be the ingathering when *she* could not enjoy it.

For they would all come, she knew, when Lizzie or Henry would send the telegrams, just as they had come before. If she could but have them all with her *now*, just once, while she could see them, talk to them, listen to them; if she could go to sleep one night, knowing that they all lay in their old childhood rooms, then the rest wouldn't matter.

Today, as she turned the letters over and over, the dark thought grew darker. It ate its way into her heart . . . Then slowly, miraculously, the idea came.

At first it seemed a nebulous thing that floated somewhere just out of reach. Then it gained form and gradually became her own. She was startled first by the sheer and awful boldness of it—and next by the wonder that she had not thought of it before, so easily and naturally did it grow to possess her. She turned it over and over, looked at it from every side, and then, because her wise, matter-of-fact old brain loved even yet to find the way out of a difficulty, Mother gave a soft, low chuckle.

She was in high spirits at supper. Lizzie brought her "near" glasses, and she read them the children's letters. Lizzie thumbed critically the sample of Laura's evening dress.

"Don't say anything about comin', any of them," remarked Henry.

"No," said Mother complacently; "but they might come before long."

That night Mother lay awake for a long time and counted her fingers. When the old clock struck twelve, she had succeeded in assigning one word to each, including thumbs. She fell asleep contentedly.

In the morning the usual program was for her to stay in bed while Lizzie and Henry did the milking. That over, and Lizzie back in the kitchen, she was at liberty to get up and dress for breakfast. This particular morning Mother wakened early and listened sharply for the rattle of milk cans and pails. At last it came; then Henry's heavy clatter down the steps of the back porch, followed by Lizzie's lighter ones; then quiet.

Mother got out of bed carefully, wrapped a blanket around her shoulders and walked across the hall to the sitting-room. Against one wall was fastened the oak box which appertains to country line telephones. Mother counted her fingers again, nervously, and then rang the bell. It took three rings to arouse Central to an answering "Hello."

"Give me Western Union," said Mother.

By the time the telegraph operator answered, Mother's knees were shaking ominously, but she clung to the receiver. She gave six addresses slowly, carefully.

"Now I want this telegram sent to each one of them. You ready? Well, this is it:

"Come for Mother's funeral Thursday. Will meet Wednesday evening train. Lizzie"

Yes, that's right. And charge them to 'phone 14, ring 22, New Salem."

It was done. Mother sat down triumphantly in her room. Now for Lizzie and Henry! She dressed tremblingly. She *was* a bit nervous. She told them at breakfast what she had done. Lizzie screamed, and began volubly to decide upon other contradictory telegrams which must be sent at once. Mother looked piteously from one to the other. Lizzie was so strong and determined. At last Henry raised his voice.

"Dogged if I don't believe you're right, Mother!" (He and Lizzie always called her that). "I guess we'll just let the thing stand, now it's done. When you get 'em here you can explain it all out to 'em."

By the time the breakfast dishes were cleared away she and Lizzie were intent upon the preparations which were to be made. After breathless debate it was decided to have the young turkey for Thursday dinner, and ham the night they arrived. Mother begged to be allowed to make some of her famous ginger cookies, and finally compromised by sitting close to Lizzie and giving her minute instructions as she mixed the ingredients and beat them with a stout right arm.

Sweet, savory smells of all kinds filled the big rooms and the high hall as the day wore on, and the whole house thrilled to a bustling, happy expectancy. Mother drew long, satisfied breaths. It would be a real reunion this time. She wondered if it would have been better to wait till Thanksgiving. But at eighty—she sighed. It was probably better as it was.

"Do you think the in-laws will come?" inquired Lizzie once.

"No," said Mother calmly; "I don't think so. They didn't to

Father's, and I really hope they don't. They're all so fine they sort of scare me. I just want the children by themselves."

By Wednesday afternoon the house from top to bottom was in readiness. The table had been extended to its old full length, and now with the best tablecloth and the "good" dishes presented a festive appearance. Mother herself set down the little blue pickle dish.

Henry, in his Sunday suit, started to the train at four. He drove the carriage and Sims was to take the buggy down and leave it for two of the boys to drive back in. That was the way they had managed when they came for Father's funeral.

Lizzie was flustered. She ran from kitchen to dining-room and back again, stopping frequently to exhort, "Now, Mother, you'll be sick. Now do go an' set down. You can't do anything to help now. Everything's ready. Now, Mother, you mind, you'll be sick!"

Mother went at last and began to watch the windows. At exactly five-thirty the two vehicles appeared above the corn-field, and her heart began to give queer, smothering jumps.

It had been arranged that Henry was to prepare the children a little before they quite reached the house. Neither ideas nor speech came to Henry quickly, so all he'd been able to manage was, "You might get a surprise. Now, I'm not sayin', but you might." This mystifying statement, repeated several times, coupled with his general evasiveness to all questions on the way, made the children watch the door with quiet fearfulness as they alighted at the gate.

Mother, watching through the slender glass panel at the side of the front door, eyed them eagerly. They were all there. They were coming up the walk. Two smartly tailored women in their early forties; four well-dressed men in their late forties and early fifties. The children! All here at last!

When they reached the porch, Lizzie threw wide the door and revealed Mother in her black silk and cameo brooch, one of the girls' lace handkerchiefs clutched nervously in one hand, another carefully tucked in her belt. She smiled on them, her eyes full of happy tears as she opened her arms wide.

"It's all right," she assured them before they had time to speak; "I ain't a ghost. I'm just as well as can be. I'll explain all about it. My, to think you're all here!"

She was drawing them to her, but their faces were amazed; they kissed her mechanically, and then the storm of questions broke. Through the babel of inquiry Howard's voice rose sternly: "For heaven's sake, Mother, how did those telegrams come to be sent?"

"Why," Mother began with a pleased smile, "I sent them. No, Lizzie didn't have a thing to do with them. No, I haven't been sick. I just had such a longing to have you all here together once, and I thought that was the only way to bring you. I'm that pleased I don't know what to do that you've all come. Henry killed the young turkey, and we're going to have one real visit. It'll be a sort of birthday party instead of a funeral." Mother laughed a little happy, broken laugh, but no one joined her.

Laura sank down on the lower stair in an attitude of despair.

"And my house full of paper hangers, and cards out for a bridge luncheon next week, and I *recalled* them!" she wailed.

"Bridge luncheon!" exclaimed Joe. "I left a ten-thousand-dollar deal to come, and I'll lose every cent of it."

"Never was so busy in my life. Just working up a new lecture and two articles that *have* to be ready next week."

"I tell you, you don't know—"

Mother stood a little apart, listening, while the light died slowly out of her eyes. They were not talking to her. They were busy explaining to each other in rather strident tones at what tremendous cost and inconvenience to themselves they had come. It did not seem to occur to any of them to be glad that the implication of the telegram was not true. At last Alice, at sight of Mother's face, raised a warning finger.

"Shh—" she whispered. "We're here now, and we must make the best of it and not worry Mother. Remember, she's eighty, and her mind may not be quite as clear as it was."

Mother did not hear the words, but in the small lull which followed she put in quaveringly, "We fixed up your old rooms for you. You mind, don't you? Laura and Alice over my room, Joe and Howard over the kitchen, and Wesley and John above the sitting-room. Just go right up, and then supper'll be ready. You'll find water in the pitchers, and towels and soap, and just make yourselves right at home."

Plain, homely old words were all that came, when her heart seemed bursting between the yearning love for them and the dull fear that all was not well. If they were angry with her, she would not be able to bear it. She went back to the dining-room and made nervous attempts to straighten the dishes on the tables, managing always to get in the path of Lizzie, who under the high excitement of six guests at once was growing more and more flushed of face and loud of tone.

"Now, Mother, you go an' set down. You're just dodderin' around in my way. You'll go and get sick because of it, and then what'll you do!"

Mother sat down feebly, and did not rise again until they

were all there ready for supper. Henry, stooping to see the extreme top of his head in the small kitchen mirror, gave a last slow stroke of the comb, and slouched into his place at the foot of the table. Lizzie "waited."

There was a faint general expansiveness of the men under the influence of the rich brown coffee and home-cured ham. But, even so, Mother watching anxiously, eating little, sensed a strange aloofness in the children's attitude toward her. Alice and Laura talked a little to her and a great deal to each other. But the boys, each full of his own interests and eager to dilate upon them to his brothers, dealt in long strange words and meaningless sentences, and apparently forgot her.

She raised her voice once, with her eyes upon Joe.

"Do you mind the time you fell off the pear tree and broke your arm?"

There had to be several efforts made by the girls to gain Joe's attention from the problem of high finance he was discussing, before the question got through. His answer was pleasant but brief, and he was soon back in his own world again.

Once more Mother tried.

"Do you mind, Howard, how you used to slip the lid off the cookie crock when you came from school and think I wouldn't hear you? These are the same kind you're eating now—my ginger cookies."

Howard seemed to have difficulty in remembering.

At the end of the meal, Joe took out his time-table and studied it carefully: "Could you get me to the junction for that eight-ten express tomorrow morning, Henry?"

Henry gave an indistinct affirmative, glancing at Mother under his brows. Mother leaned forward.

"Joe, you ain't going *tomorrow* morning?"

"Why, yes, Mother, I must. You see, this little joke of yours is going to be a pretty expensive one for me, and the sooner I can get back, the better."

There followed a general scanning of time-tables by the boys. It seemed that though their directions were different, they could all get trains near the same time. Mother's face looked stricken.

"Boys, you ain't *all* going in the morning. Why—why, we're *having the turkey!*"

Howard spoke with the kind firmness with which one would reprove a child.

"You see, Mother, we're all busy men. We have important affairs to look after. If you had been ill, or—or anything serious had happened, we would willingly have put everything else aside to come; but when you are well and comfortable it was very wrong of you to deceive us as you did. I know it's hard for you away off here in the country to understand just how busy we all are, but you must try to realize it."

Now, Mother began to realize many things. She realized that she was chided, rebuked; that she was old and very, very tired. She sat quiet during the rest of the evening, while the children talked.

At nine she went to her room. The boys repeated rather heavily, as if saying a lesson, that they were sorry they must go, of course, and miss that turkey—but business was business—so busy—would see her for a minute in the morning before they left. The girls came in to say good night after she was in bed. They were both tender, but Laura's attitude indicated that she'd not entirely forgotten her postponed bridge party.

"I'll stay until tomorrow evening, Mother, then I simply must go back. You know how it is with paper hangers in the house and no one to oversee them but the children. Oh, I left things in such a state! It makes me wild to think of it! Well, good night, Mother; get a good sleep."

Mother was too weary to lie awake and think.

The clock on the mantel was striking two long, sonorous strokes when she woke. She tried to turn over. A strange weight seemed to have settled upon her body. She was frightened. She tried to call Lizzie in the next room. She could make no sound. *Then she knew.* She was going as she had wished to go, as Father had gone, quietly in the night time. It was all right.

Then, groping hazily, her brain searched through a clouded consciousness for the outlines of a dull distress that lay upon it. *There had been trouble*, she remembered vaguely.

Then it came back terrifyingly. *The children were displeased with her.* The remembrance all at once was surprisingly clear. Her sending the telegrams, their coming, their irritation and words of reproof.

Then, clearer still, for one brief second, the new comfort came. *There would now be no deception. It would all come true, and, being true, she would be forgiven.*

Then three long massive strokes came—and Mother lay very still.

In their childhood rooms, the children slept on.

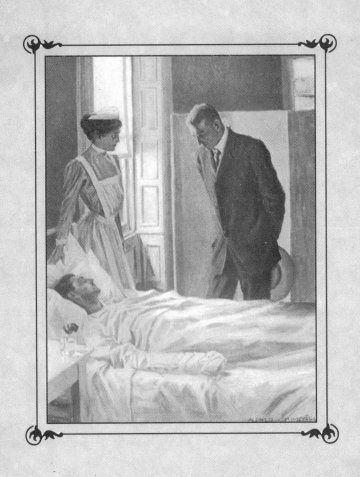

STORY OF LOVE

AUTHOR UNKNOWN

Yes, her baby was perfect ... except for ...
So was the child's life to be ruined?

"May I see my baby!" the happy new mother asked. When the little bundle was nestled in her arms and she moved the fold of cloth to look upon his tiny face, she gasped. The doctors turned quickly and looked out the tall hospital window. The baby had been born without ears.

Time proved that the boy's hearing was perfect. It was only his appearance that was marred. When he rushed home from school one day and flung himself into his mother's arms, she sighed, knowing that his life was to be a succession of sobs. "I got into a fight—I didn't mean to!" he blurted out the tragedy. "A boy, a big boy, called me—a freak!"

He grew up, handsome except for his misfortune. A favorite with his fellow-students, he might have been class president, but—for that. He developed poetic gifts, a talent for literature and music. "But you must mingle with other young people," his mother reproved him, and felt a tightness in her heart.

The boy's father had a session with the family physician. Could nothing be done? "I believe I could graft on a pair of outer ears, if they could be procured," the doctor concluded. Whereupon the search began for a person who would make such a sacrifice for a young man with his life ahead of him.

The days dragged wearily into two years. Then: "You are going to the hospital, son! Mother and I have found someone. But it's a deep secret," said the father to his surprised son.

The operation was brilliantly successful, and a new person emerged. His talents blossomed into genius and school and college became an unbroken series of triumphs. Later he married and entered the diplomatic service.

"But I *must* know!" he urged his father. "Who gave so much for me? I could never do enough for that person!"

"I do not believe you could," said his father. "But the agreement was that you are not to know—not yet."

The years kept their profound secret, but the day *did* come—one of the darkest days that ever a son passes through. He stood with his father, bowed over his mother's casket.

Slowly, tenderly, the father stretched forth a hand and raised the thick, reddish-brown hair, to reveal—that the mother had no outer ears!

"Mother said she was glad she had never let her hair be cut," he whispered . . . "And nobody ever thought Mother less beautiful, did they?"

BEAUTIFUL DREAMER

ARTHUR GORDON

The young writer was broke, so much so that his wife took the children with her to her folks' place for a while. Without them, he was desolate. So that night he went down to the auction house.

Then in came a young man and his expectant wife in an almost desperate search for a cheap baby buggy—but they didn't have enough money.

Life would never be the same again for the young writer after that night.

You know, when things are going pretty well at last, and the pressure is off, and you're not frightened anymore, sometimes you look back. You look back at all the misery and uncertainty, at the times when it was really rough, when you didn't think you could keep going for another day or even another hour. You expect to feel a great relief.

But you don't. You feel a kind of sadness—almost a sort of regret—a sense of loss rather than gain. Because you begin to realize that those times—grim though they were—had a vividness, a reality far more intense than the easier present. And it takes only a word, or a gesture, or a few notes from an old song to bring it all flooding back . . .

We were broke that summer, good and broke. I had worked up enough courage to quit the magazine and try free-lancing, but I underestimated the length of time it takes to get started. Also, when you're scared you tighten up and write badly. We kept the show on the road by selling a few things—household things—at the outdoor auction on the edge of town. But that was all we did sell, and finally it got to the point where Pam decided to take the children to visit their grandmother for a while. We hadn't quarreled, or anything. It was just a question of debts, and of paying for the groceries.

She left early one morning, and I think that was the longest day of my life. I tried to work, but it was no good; the house was too quiet and empty. I kept telling myself I didn't have to endure all this; that all I had to do was call the magazine and ask for my old job back. I was pretty sure I'd get it. In the end, it wasn't courage that kept me from making the call. It was lack of it. I didn't have the nerve to admit that I had failed.

The sun went down and the twilight was gray with loneliness. When it was fully dark, I decided to walk down to the auction and sell a suitcase I had. Pam had a birthday coming up and I wanted to buy her a present.

It wasn't much of a place, really, just a big shed full of junk, and a tent with folding chairs where people came to bid for things you'd have thought nobody could possibly want. Secondhand things, castoffs—even broken things.

The owner was a hard-bitten little gnome named Willie Madden who looked at the world suspiciously from under a green eyeshade and from behind a dead cigar. He and Pam had gotten pretty chummy over our previous transactions, but I didn't like him much.

I arranged to have the suitcase auctioned. Then, since there was an hour to kill, I prowled around looking at the old furniture and chipped china and musty books. And finally, near the back of the shed, I noticed a couple standing close together and whispering about something.

They were not a very striking pair; neither of them was tall and the girl wasn't particularly pretty. But there was something nice and close about them. They were inspecting a secondhand baby carriage, and it was obvious that before long they were going to need one.

"Well, go and ask him," the girl said, loud enough for me to hear. "You can *ask*, can't you?"

The boy nodded and went away. While he was gone, the

girl stood looking down at the carriage. In its prime it had been quite a fancy affair, and it was still in good condition. I saw her stroke the ivory handle gently, and once she bent and reexamined the price tag, as if she hoped somehow her first impression of what it read had been wrong.

Her husband came back presently with Willie Madden. Willie grunted at me from under his eyeshade, then went over and looked at the tag himself. "That's right," he said. "Twenty-five bucks. An absolute steal at that price, too. It's worth fifty."

The girl asked a question, her face wistful as she looked at the carriage.

"Well, bring it in, bring it in," Willie said impatiently. "Bring in anything you want to get rid of. But you better hurry. I got to be up on that platform in just forty-five minutes."

The youngsters hurried away, but in twenty minutes they were back. I watched them go up to Willie's cluttered desk and put down the things they were carrying: a fishing rod, a couple of dresses, an alarm clock, and a few other odds and ends including something that looked like a music box. It didn't look like twenty-five dollars' worth of auctionable stuff to me, and I knew it didn't to Willie. He poked at the music box with one skeptical finger. "This thing work?"

"It plays one tune," the girl said. "It's supposed to play three but it plays one."

Willie's cigar revolved slowly. "I paid twenty-two bucks for that carriage. Here it is, right in the book. If we can get that much for this stuff of yours, you can have it. But I tell you right now, I don't think you'll get that much. So don't say I didn't warn you. Go on, now; wait in the tent. I got things to do."

They went, and I followed them. I sat where I could watch their faces. They held hands and waited.

Somebody got a good buy on my suitcase; it went for fourteen dollars, and was worth forty. The youngsters' things were at the end of the list; it was late when Willie got around to them. The fishing rod brought three dollars, the dresses two each, the alarm clock, fifty cents. It was hopeless, absolutely hopeless. I tried not to look at them.

Willie picked up the music box. "Now this here," he said, "is a genuine antique. What's more, it really plays. Listen."

He pressed the lever. The box gave a faint purring sound; then it played. The song was Stephen Foster's "Beautiful Dreamer." It came tinkling out, slow and sad, the most haunting of all American folk songs, maybe of folk songs anywhere:

> *Beautiful dreamer, wake unto me,*
> *Starlight and dewdrop are waiting for thee.*

The tent was very still. The music went on, thin and clear and sweet, and somehow everything was in it—all the loneliness and the heartache and the things all of us want to say and never find the words. I looked at the young couple, and something in their faces made my throat feel tight.

The music stopped. "Well, " said Willie, "what am I bid? Ten dollars? Anyone bid ten dollars?"

Silence again. I thought of the fourteen dollars I would be getting for my suitcase. Less commission. I thought about Pam and her birthday, too.

"Anybody bid five?" Willie sounded impatient. "Anybody bid five dollars for this genuine antique?"

I took a deep breath, opened my mouth and then miserably closed it again.

"Five dollars!" said a voice behind me. I looked around. It was a thin, shabby man with a carefully waxed mustache. I had seen him at auctions before, but I had never heard him bid on anything.

Even Willie seemed rather surprised, "Fi-dollazime bid . . . who'll make it ten? Ten dollars? Who'll make it eight?"

"Eight!" It was a little birdlike woman on the far side of the tent.

Every eye in the place swung back to the shabby man. He did not even hesitate. "Ten dollars!"

"Twelve!" cried his rival. She looked as if she didn't have twelve cents.

"*Twelve* I'm bid," yelled Willie. "Do I hear fifteen?"

There was a hush that seemed to go on forever. Fifteen dollars would do it for them, plus the money from their other things. The girl was very pale; she was holding her husband's hand so tightly that I saw him wince.

The shabby man stood up slowly. "Fifteen dollars!" he said with grand finality.

That did it. The music box was going—it was gone—*sold* to the gentleman with the mustache. For a moment the grim thought occurred to me that the gentleman might not have fifteen dollars. But no, he produced the money, gave it to Willie's assistant, took the box.

When the tent was empty, I went back into the shed. The baby carriage, I was glad to note, was gone. I collected my suitcase money and decided to treat myself to a cup of coffee. The truth was I didn't want to go back to my empty house. I went into the diner across the street and stopped just inside the door. The little birdlike lady and her rival with the mustache were sitting there, side by side, on a couple of stools.

I understood the whole thing, then. I went up to them and said sharply, as if I had a right to know, "Where's the music box?"

The owner of the mustache looked faintly startled. "The box?" he said. "Why, Willie's got it."

I turned to his companion. "How much did Willie pay you to bid against each other?"

She dunked a doughnut daintily. "Why, nothing," she said. "We were glad to do it, weren't we, Henry?"

"I suppose," I said, "that it was Willie's money you used to pay for it, too."

"Sure," said Henry. "Where would I get fifteen bucks for a music box? Willie just hates for people to know what a softie he is, that's all."

I left them there and went back to the shed where Willie sat at his desk. I guess he wore that eyeshade to make himself look tough. "Where's the box?" I asked.

He stared me right in the eye. "What box?"

"Come on, Willie," I said. "I know what you did. Where is it?"

The eyeshade moved an inch to the left. "In the cupboard there. Why?"

"I want you to hold it for me. I'll give you twenty bucks for it when I have the money."

Willie leaned back in his chair. "Now just what," he said, "would you do with that box?"

"I'd give it to Pam for her birthday."

Willie shook his head. "Are you crazy? It's not worth five

bucks, let alone twenty. It only plays one tune. It's supposed to play three."

"I like the tune it does play," I told him. "There's a lot of love in it."

"Love?" said Willie. He got up slowly and came around the desk. He looked at me balefully. "Why don't you get a job and do some work for a change? Why don't you quit this fool way of living?"

I just laughed out loud. I felt happy and warm and good inside. I knew that sooner or later everything would be all right.

Willie opened the cupboard. "Here." He held out the box. "Give it to Pam. On her birthday. From me."

I hesitated for a second; then I took it. There are times when it's selfish to refuse a gift. "Thanks."

"Well, go on home," said Willie. "I can't stand around here all night talking."

So I went home. The house was still dark and empty, but I put the box on the table by our bed. I put it there, and I let it play, and I wasn't lonely anymore.

THE LITTLE ROOM

AUTHOR UNKNOWN

*T*hings were awfully quiet in the Crane farmhouse. Ever since little Andy had died, things had been different. In fact, it sometimes seemed as if they had ceased to really live seven years ago.

And then came a knock at the door.

Farmer Crane's dining room presented a homey picture in the radiance of the kerosene lamp. Farmer Crane himself relaxed in his favorite armchair, dozing.

Eunice Crane, her low, cushioned rocker drawn close to the grate, turned the socks she had finished mending and smiled wistfully.

Steve drops off to sleep so easily, she thought. *I suppose it's the hard outdoor work he does all day long that makes him sleepy in the evenings. It's kind of lonesome, though, sitting here with not a sound to break the silence. If little Andy had lived he would have been the life of the old house now.*

Eunice Crane had fallen into the habit of musing about Andy, wondering if Stephen would not have been different if the boy had lived, instead of dropping out of their existence just at an age when he had become the center of all their thoughts. It had been a bitter blow to the two, and instead of drawing them closer together, they had emerged from the depths of their grief hardened, and with a shadow between them that even the long years had not driven away.

Eunice would have liked to live on in the shadow of little Andy's brief existence. She would have liked to talk a little now and then about Andy's sayings, and the things Andy had done.

But in those first days of their anguish, Stephen, with a bitter look in his eyes, had harshly stopped her every allusion to Andy. For seven years the halls of the old farm house had not heard the patter of childish feet, nor the big rooms re-echo with boyish laughter. A silence, oppressive and lonely, had settled down upon their evenings.

If Stephen would only take an interest in some one else's boy, they might spend many an evening planning for him. There was Cousin Sally Derling's boy, just about a year older than Andy. But, there! It would take a miracle to arouse Stephen's interest in Cousin Sally's boy, for he wasn't Andy. She realized now that it had been a selfish affection which they had expended on Andy: they had no eyes for any other child than their own.

"Rap, rap, rap!" sounded the old knocker.

Eunice came back to the present with a start, and Stephen Crane's nodding person jerked upright with a suddenness from the fender on which his foot had been resting.

"I declare!" he exclaimed, yawning.

Eunice pushed back her rocker and hurried to the kitchen door. As she opened it, she caught a glimpse of a boy's figure standing in the darkness of the porch.

"Good evening. Is this the Warner place?" questioned a clear, ringing voice.

"The Warner place? Why, no, laddie, this is the old Crane homestead. The Warner place is—Come inside until I ask Stephen," commanded Eunice, holding the door open. The boy accepted her invitation and followed her into the dining room.

"Stephen, isn't Warner the name of the man who bought Joe Grayson's place?" she questioned.

"Why—er—yes. He's a stranger to these parts. It's three miles across to the old Grayson place. Boy, you're a long piece out of your way."

Eunice Crane turned questioningly to the lad. She noticed

the fearless brown eyes, the shock of black hair, and the ruddy cheeks glowing with the long tramp.

"I can't see how I came to get so mixed up," pondered the boy. "The fellow who runs the mail said to follow the Neck Road till I came to the lane of cherry trees. He said I'd find the folk I was looking for in the big, white house with a green latticed front porch."

Farmer Crane started. "Well, now, that's strange. Benny Stokes as runs the mail knows us too well to misdirect you. Seems as if he must have misunderstood ye, some way."

The lad shook his head. "Can you tell me the way to the Warner place? If I don't get a hustle on, I'm scared they will be to bed when I get there, and I'll have to stay outdoors all night. There's a storm coming up, too."

"I should say there was!" exclaimed Eunice. "You never could make your way across the fields this time of night, for the marsh is flooded, isn't it Stephen?"

"Sure, the marsh is flooded, and you'd only get lost on it tonight. I guess you'd better put up here until morning. How'd you happen to be lookin' for the Warners, and where do you hail from?" Stephen questioned.

"A man on the Neck, where I came from, told me they were looking for a boy on Warner's place, an' I'm looking for a job. My dad died a month ago. Some of the neighbors took the three girls and will give them homes, but I'm big enough to look out for myself."

"And your mother?" questioned Eunice.

"Oh, she died so long ago I don't remember much about her."

"What are you going to work at over at the Warner's?" questioned Stephen.

"The man who told me about the job said Mr. Warner wanted a smart boy to learn how to run his farm machinery." The brown eyes snapped. "I'd sure like that kind of job," he declared.

"Wife, can you put this chap up for the night? By the way, what's your name?" he asked.

"Davy Starr, sir. I'd be much obliged if you could keep me for tonight. Maybe there is something I can do to pay you."

"Tut, tut!" laughed Stephen.

A smile radiated from Eunice Crane's face. Her woman's heart longed for that homeless boy, to mother him as if he had been her own.

Out in the hall and up the stairway she went to prepare a sleeping place for the lad.

When she came back to the dining room the boy was gone. Questioningly she looked into Stephen's face.

"He seemed anxious for something to do, so I give him a basket an' a lantern and sent him down in the cellar for some pippins," he answered.

The boy's step sounded on the stairs. Stephen Crane cleared his throat. "Where are ye puttin' him to sleep, Eunice?" he asked.

"In the little room," she admitted. It was there Andy had slept, and it had never been used since Andy had gone.

Eunice took the basket from Davy's hands, and wiping the apples, piled the old fruit dish high with them. Accepting an apple, the boy sat down again by the hearth.

"How did it happen that cherry trees border the lane?" the boy asked.

"Well, you see," and Stephen began with the story of how

his forefathers had settled the farm, and the wide-awake interest of the boy spurred him on.

When the clock struck the hour of ten, Stephen started,
"My goodness, how the evening's gone. It's time young folks
was goin' to bed."

Eunice laughed softly, "I guess it's past bedtime. Haven't
you any bundle with you?" she questioned.

"I hadn't any clothes worth carrying," he explained, following her into the hall as she indicated she would show him
to his room.

Then, turning, he called back, "Good night, sir! You ought
to be proud of Cherry Lane, a place that's got stories away back
about the trees growing on it. I'm sure glad I stopped over
tonight at your place."

Up the stairs he followed. Eunice had hunted out a night-
shirt of Stephen's, and Davy put it on, but he almost drowned
in it—because it was so big, and he was so small. Tucking him
in and assuring herself of his comfort, with a tremulous good
night on her lips, she picked up the lamp, moved toward the
door, and picking up the boy's trousers carried them over her
arm downstairs. Sitting down in the rocker and threading a
needle, she began to darn the frayed edges.

"Steve, ain't we heard strange stories about the Warner
man?" questioned Eunice.

Stephen stirred the coals before he answered.

"There's all kinds of rumors goin' around. He's not the
kind of man I'd want to entrust a boy of mine, that's for sure.
When he is in liquor, he's very abusive. Davy is a clean boy
now, and has no bad habits, but a few years with that man
might be his ruin. He's got a long head on him to take this

husky, wide-awake youngster. He'll work him, too, and don't you forget it!"

"But, Steve, he'll work him to death," protested Eunice.

"Yes, that's the trouble—he'll break him; and if he gets brutal, there ain't any womankind exceptin' the hired hand to interfere."

"Steve, would he be likely to beat Davy?"

"Well, now, I'm not the one to judge, but, as I said, I wouldn't want a boy of mine to—do—" Stephen's voice trailed into a husky muttering.

"But can't we do something to prevent his going to Warner's, Steve?"

"We better look the ground over. Would it bother you to have him around for a couple of days?" he asked.

"No trouble at all," she answered.

She finished patching the boy's trousers and led the way upstairs.

Stephen went downstairs again to lock the storm door, and quietly she stole along the hall to the little room. Dropping on her knees by the bedside, she laid her cheek against his cheek. The boy stirred, and she noiselessly stole back to her own room.

For several days Stephen drove about making inquiries about the man Warner.

"I find no good word of Warner, and from what I've seen of him at his place, he'd soon make an old man of Davy. It ain't no place for him, and I'll hunt him a better one."

The boy was ever at his heels, running about the farm, waking up the old house with boyish mirth, and filling Eunice Crane's heart with the joy that Andy's boyishness would have brought her. The weeks merged into months, and Stephen had still found no place he considered worthy of Davy.

Early in May, Stephen came home from the village. Eunice read dejection on his face. "Is the boy around?" he queried.

"I—I've found a place for him with Alf Gates. He will take him into his family, and his wife will be good to the lad. I suppose it will rid you of looking after him."

"I suppose it's been quite a worry to you, we've lived so quiet like," she answered.

Quietly, at the usual hour they went to bed.

"The rheumatism's pretty bad in my shoulder; guess I better get the liniment," he remarked.

Eunice went across the hall to the little room, dropped on her knees, and laying her cheek against the boy's, she pressed her lips again and again on his cheek, and the tears so long repressed fell on the pillow.

"Davy, boy, I cannot give you up," she cried. "It is just as if Andy had grown into a boy, and they were taking him away again," she sobbed.

Suddenly she was conscious of sobs on the other side of the pillow.

"Mother! Mother!" it was Stephen's voice crying out to her. "It fair breaks my heart to give up the boy. It's like giving up my own! But I feared you were against keepin' him and letting him have Andy's place."

"It's been a taste of heaven having him in the old house!" exclaimed Eunice. "But I worried for fear he was a burden you."

Suddenly the supposedly sleeping boy cried out with excitement: "Oh, and now I can stay forever and ever, and you'll be my very own mother?"

"Your own mother never loved you more than I shall," exclaimed Eunice, holding him close.

Stephen's arm reached out around the woman and the boy. "I guess there won't be no trouble takin' out papers. How'd you like it, sonny, if we fix it up so you can take our name, and Cherry Lane will be your own when we are through with it?"

Davy reached up and kissed the rough, unshaven cheek, and snuggled down contentedly in the warm bed.

Next Sunday found Stephen and Eunice with Davy in the Crane pew at church.

At the close of the service Benny Stokes came to the Crane pew. "What's this, Steve, I hear about you taking out adoption papers for this boy?"

"Well, it ain't just a rumor; it is the real truth," explained Stephen.

Davy pushed through into the aisle, smiling as he said: "It's true my name is David Crane, and I belong to Cherry Lane, and she's my mother."

Eunice smiled through misty tears into Davy's happy face.

"Well, I reckon I didn't do such a bad thing, after all, when I misdirected the boy to Cherry Lane, now, did I?" questioned Benny Stokes. "I knew he was a steady, honest boy, and worthy of a good home," he went on with a mysterious smile.

THE NEW NEIGHBOR

EMMA GARY WALLACE

Invite the famous author to attend a study group? Preposterous! She'd laugh at everyone. Better to leave well enough alone.

So . . . the lady invited herself.

The Howland house had stood vacant for more than a year, and we had never got used to the lonesome and inhospitable appearance of curtainless windows showing stark and empty rooms beyond.

The garden had grown up in a single season to a tangle of weeds, and the paths were disconsolately overgrown. So we were all delighted on Maple Street when we heard that the house had been leased and a family would move in immediately. We were even more pleased when we learned that the new mistress of the home was none other than a well-known writer on home and home-making topics.

It was going to be great to have her in our neighborhood, and we who lived there experienced an eager hope that she would be willing to be one of us.

"Just think of all the help and the inspiration she can be to us, if she only will," I said again and again to John—my better half. "It will be perfectly wonderful to have a really and truly authoress in our midst! Don't you think so?"

John's eyes twinkled.

"I don't doubt but what you are right," he grinned back, "but I am also thinking that with a live wide-awake bunch like this Maple Street crowd—that the inspiration may be as much for her as for you. Writer folk, you know, have to keep in touch with the actual happenings of life, in order to be able to give out to others, or their material will not ring true, nor will it prove helpful and vital. So, Honey, don't get the inferiority complex. Probably this local lioness will be as ready to neighbor as you will be to neighbor with her.

"And by the way, did you plan to ask her to join that Sunday School class of yours about which you're always talking? I should think that kind of a woman would find such a group meat and drink in the way of mental stimulus."

I hadn't thought of asking Mrs. Washburn, the newcomer, to become a member of our class group, and to be perfectly honest, now that John suggested it, I found myself hanging back and making all sorts of excuses to myself.

Perhaps she didn't belong to our denomination, and if she did, would our simple and practical talks on the problems we considered from week to week interest her? Or would they sound almost childish to a woman of whom we thought of as dealing with big affairs?

Would a woman of her education and standing prove something of a check on the spontaneity and freedom of speech of such women as constituted our members?

There was little Mrs. Cato with her three fine children who were doing so well, yet Alice Cato had never gone through high school and often made rather startling grammatical errors. And independent little Mrs. Seels was a trifle radical and inclined to be a bit eccentric in her opinions.

And how would a broad-minded woman like Mrs. Washburn look upon our Mrs. Chester, who always saw the opposite side of questions—a side to which the rest of us usually seemed to have been blind. And more often than not Mrs. Chester could put up a mighty good argument in support of her own ideas. She was a minister's daughter, and slightly embittered by a life of unusual harshness and injustice which seemed to have followed her from the time she left the parental roof.

We all understood each other and loved each other dearly, and I couldn't help but wonder whether a woman such as I expected Mrs. Washburn to be would fit in. Would she not be a sort of foreign body in our midst?

The very thought was displeasing, for we had found so much of genuine helpfulness in our earnest study and discussion of our lesson problems. We had always been singularly free to speak, and to give our candid opinions and to abide by the Bible teachings on the subject under discussion, and it was amazing, we found, how often we discovered that we had always overlooked important evidence which we had not taken into consideration at all.

Personally, I had gone into that class thinking myself rather wise, only to discover in the course of time that I had often been decidedly one-sided and even intolerant.

Yes, it gave me a little jolt to think of Mrs. Washburn and what she might think of us. Perhaps she would look upon us as not quite up to the standard of thought of the big city where she had lived.

When the lady in question finally arrived, I was desperately anxious to get a peep at her, and I was interested to find her tall and stately, and while I wouldn't describe her as handsome, there was really something very beautiful and queenly about her carriage and the graciousness of her smile.

She didn't wait for me to call, but promptly scraped acquaintance across the dividing hedge when she saw me out hanging up some muslin which I had dipped in water and was putting on the line to shrink.

But a shadow fell across that first interview. It was the conviction I felt that I was going to be too cowardly to take her to our class. Here we dealt with the everyday problems of the training of our children, and the solving of our own difficulties in the light of the special lesson problem we were studying.

You see, our class endeavored to get as much personal help each week as we could from the consideration of the Bible text and our own conferences. We all knew each other—and, well, it was just a little disturbing to take a Queen Marie sort of a woman into our group.

Several weeks went by, and Mrs. Washburn and I had become very congenial friends—enough so that she ran in quite often, and one day I propounded to her the class problem for the week, which was one concerning the measure and extent of personal responsibility. In a minute we were in animated discussion, and it was evident that mentally she was keen and searching.

"I should like to go to that class of yours," she exclaimed, "for it must be perfectly splendid to bring out both sides of practical problems as you say you do, and if you ask me, I know that I shall accept your invitation promptly.

"You see, I haven't been going to church for a number of years. There were reasons at first, and when the pathway was cleared up so that I might have gone, I had lost interest. Of course I attend special services now and again as inclination prompts, but I rather think I have become a sort of religious tramp. Possibly I'll find anchorage now that we have come to this lovely little town to live."

After that, what could I do but ask her to go with me, and so the next Sunday I had the pleasure of introducing Mrs. Washburn to the women of our group. A few of them had met her, but most of them had not, although naturally they had heard of her.

It was a relief that she should take her place as simply as any ordinary woman. But my peace of mind was not to last long, for Mrs. Chester was never more than a few minutes in probing courteously, the major interest of any person whom she met.

"I hope," exclaimed Mrs. Chester, "that you have children like the rest of us, for that makes us all more sympathetic to the shortcomings of the offspring of the rest, and more helpful in our practical applications."

"I have a son," responded Mrs. Washburn, "but he is no longer at home."

In a flash I saw that Mrs. Chester had unwittingly touched something very painful, for Mrs. Washburn's face hardened, and even lost something of its fresh bloom, taking on instead a gray, tired look.

Perhaps it was intuition, but I assumed then and there that the poor soul was unhappy about that boy. Perhaps he was not living the life she would have, or there was an estrangement.

It happened that our regular teacher was away, and I was taking her place, so I tried to steer the discussion into safe channels. Mrs. Washburn was an attentive listener and only spoke once or twice when directly appealed to, but I was sure she was interested.

It was rather unlike her, however, that she didn't refer to that discussion, or to her estimate of the class appeal on the way home or during the following week.

The next Sunday, however, she was waiting and went along with me. The discussion centered about the great patience of God in refraining many times from speedy and severe punishment, though merited, thus giving His children an opportunity to see for themselves how mistaken and willful they have been.

It was Mrs. Cato who brought out the thought that this sort of watchful waiting on the part of the Heavenly Father is not indifference or a sign that He no longer cares for us, but rather a demonstration of His great loving kindness and patience, for even as He gave Naomi an excuse to leave the heathen land of Moab and to go back to her old neighborhood in Judea, so He is always giving us an opportunity and an open door through which to lead us back to the sunshine and warmth and comfort of His protecting presence.

We were all just a little bit startled when Mrs. Washburn spoke up with a touch of sharpness in her tone, protestingly.

"But," she said, "if you or I *know* we are right—are absolutely positive about it—are we justified in condoning evil by tolerating it? Are we not accomplices before the fact if we do that?

"Suppose, for example, that I have a daughter and she is doing things which distress me, and that I feel will lead her into wrong company and perhaps ruin her life. Shall I be patient while she defies me? And when she seizes her own way in spite of me, shall I yield to the apparently inevitable and be pleasant and tolerant with her; or shall I put my foot right down and say, 'As long as you live under my roof, you must respect my wishes or leave it.'

"And suppose"—Mrs. Washburn's breath caught—"in her stubbornness she leaves, and the home ties are broken, perhaps never to be mended. Is it not harder for the mother to go through such a test of alienation and adherence to principles, than to put on the soft pedal and compromise, and *hope* that someday things will straighten out?"

There was a silence in the class for a few minutes, and it was as clear to me as anything, that Mrs. Washburn was not speaking of a daughter, or of a hypothetical case, but rather of the son of her own heart for whom she was yearning at that minute.

"I am convinced," spoke up Mrs. Chester slowly and with almost tremulous earnestness, "that we mothers are often like I was as a child when I dug up my rosebush every day to see if the roots were actually growing. Sometimes I washed and scraped off the little roots and delicate shoots in my desire to help matters along. I killed my rose. My mother tried to tell me that Nature would do her part if I would but do mine in watering the bush and enriching the soil, and in keeping it insect-free, but I didn't listen. I thought I knew better than she.

"If I had a daughter who didn't listen to me," went on Mrs. Chester rather slowly, "I should be sure of two things. One would be that I had failed somehow in my own mother-duty and guidance and sympathy when she was in the plastic stage, and that now it was my sacred duty to be very patient with her, and so if possible to mend as far as I could, my own errors.

"The other would be that I would never accomplish anything by heated arguments and by trying to force matters as I tried to force the growth of my rose. In place of driving her away from home, I should endeavor to win her confidence and hold her by my side as closely and as long as I could, lest she be thrown into the camp of the enemy without the protection of my influence and love."

The discussion went briskly forward, our members taking different sides of the case, and bringing up different phases of it.

Mrs. Washburn said no more, but I sensed her feeling. Inwardly, she was in a turmoil—and, for some reason or other, actually suffering.

That evening she came over to me through the opening in the hedge between our two places. She flung herself into a chair in front of the fireplace where a log was burning, for the evening was cool.

"I wish I hadn't gone to that class of yours," she laughed rather bitterly, "for the way you discuss problems is disturbing, to say the least. I know I can trust you," she continued, "so I am going to spread before you one of the pages from the book of my life.

"I have been unhappy for some time. Any mother is who has lost her son—and I have lost mine. I never had a shadow of doubt but what I was in the right until last Sunday and today, and you people up at that class have quite unsettled me. I can tell you the story in a nutshell.

"Roger began to smoke cigarettes. I tried to have him stop and pointed out the harm which science declares such a habit does to body and brain. He wouldn't listen to me, although I kept at it constantly, because I felt humiliated that when I had talked and written against it, I should be powerless to control it in my own son.

"Finally, relations became strained, and one day in anger I told Roger just what I said in class today—to heed my wishes or we would live separately. He was proud. I shall never forget how white he turned when he dropped his head and left the room. I heard him packing, and later he went out of the front door without bidding me good-bye. I was listening and my impulse was to call him and to beg that we should both start over again, but I was as proud as he.

"Roger has been gone three years. I have not seen him, although I have heard from him, and I fear that he hasn't been helped by being thrust out in that manner. I never would admit it before, but today the pros and cons of that problem brought it home to me with cutting clearness. Roger hasn't forgotten, because at Christmas and on my birthday there always comes a little gift, but without a word."

The tears were running down Mrs. Washburn's face.

"And you don't know where he is?" I queried softly.

"Yes," she said, "I do, for only yesterday I received a letter from an old friend of mine and in it she said that she had met Roger unexpectedly. Great was her surprise when she went into a certain store in a strange city, to have him come forward to serve her. She mentioned the name of the store. I do not know whether it was mere happenstance or she had a purpose in it."

The tears were running down my cheeks by this time.

"I don't know either," I replied, "but I am sure of this—that God has made it easy for you and has opened the door for you to invite Roger to return."

"Then you would advise that I bring him home? He is still under age."

"I would advise," I said gently, "that you go to him and tell him the door is open, and that while you still feel the same about the habit referred to, you will leave it to his own heart to do what is right. I can see no good purpose to be served by keeping the door closed to him—the door of your heart and love. Surely your opportunity will be greater if he is within the zone of your influence. Besides you know, none of us is perfect, and yet as long as there is life and hope, our Heavenly Father gives *us* our chance."

Mrs. Washburn was standing up and her face was shining.

"It must be," she exclaimed, smiling through her tears, "that I was brought to Middletown to live that I might know you. I am going after Roger tonight. I need him and he needs me."

I took her hands in mine and it never occurred to me that she was a woman nationally known. We were just sisters and mothers.

"Oh, I am so glad," I said, "and just between ourselves, I shall go with you, with love and prayers every step of the way."

Mrs. Washburn is now the teacher of our class, and the class has doubled in size. And Roger is at home, for he has taken up his education where he dropped it, and he is leader of the Young People's Society in our church, for he has all the charm and all the candid sincerity and courage of his distinguished mother.

I tremble, however, when I think what might have been had I never invited my neighbor to go with me, and if we as a class had never discussed frankly the different sides of the many problems which we faced week by week.

Mrs. Washburn is not the only one who has seen light in hitherto dark places.

STELLA SOLARIS

JOSEPH LEININGER WHEELER

*S*tella is tired. More than tired, she's so drained by recent events that it takes almost superhuman energy to get up after only two hours' sleep, dress, load the four-wheel drive, and then stay awake down the serpentine mountain roads. It's 3:30 a.m. when she eases into a parking spot at Denver International Airport. She had no trouble finding a parking space for no one but fools venture into the skies these days.

In the terminal, military are everywhere, rifles at the ready. Since no one is used to the makeshift screening systems that are in place, everyone is edgy. It takes forever to get through security. As she finishes one of the bottles of water she brought, she thinks kind thoughts about designer socks and comfortable shoes and not-so-very-kind thoughts of fashion magazines as she sympathetically eyes the woman ahead of her wearing way too much eyeliner and impossibly high-heeled Manolo Blahniks.

Inside the aircraft, there's plenty of room to stretch out—indeed, it's half empty. As the Delta plane races down the runway and noses into the mile-high-thin air, the tension inside is palpable, each passenger thinking, *Are there any suspicious characters on board?*

The pilot doesn't level off until reaching 40,000 feet. By that time the woman is asleep.

A JOURNAL SPEAKS

Stella feels like a sleepwalker navigating through a bad dream in the Atlanta and New York terminals. As in Denver, the military, suspiciously eyeing each person in the terminal, are everywhere . . .

At JFK, security is tighter yet. Now, as the 767 lifts off the runway, passengers peer intently out the windows, hoping—yet dreading—to see the still-smoking crater where once the World Trade Center stood.

And then it is night.

The night seems endless, and sleep is long in coming. Stella awakens to see the snow-capped Alps far below and turns up the collar of her soft, cotton overshirt. From her carry-on bag, she draws out her well-worn journal. Every day since September 11, 2001, when the American world was turned upside down, she'd been faithfully chronicling thoughts and events in this book. Now, for the first time, she rereads those entries.

Three weeks ago yesterday, it had happened. Stella had finished breakfast, done the dishes, and been idly watching the morning news when she saw an airliner crash into one of the Twin Towers of New York's World Trade Center. At first she thought it must be a promo for a new movie. Certainly it could not possibly be real! Along with millions of other viewers, she witnessed another passenger airliner plunging into the second Twin Tower. Both towers were instant infernos.

So fast did event pile onto event that news broadcasters, divorced from their scripts, floundered as they tried to make some sort of sense out of what was happening. In her journal she had written what she saw:

The Twin Towers have collapsed . . . thousands dead. Another airliner has crashed into the Pentagon, and the world's largest building is in flames. Air Force One has been diverted to the Midwest, as no one knows if it is safe for the President to return to Washington. All airplanes flying towards or in American airspace have been ordered to land at the nearest airport. Military aircraft have orders to shoot down any non-military airplane that defies this order . . . Wall Street has closed. Another airliner headed for the White House or the Capitol Building crashes in Pennsylvania as heroic passengers overpower the terrorists on board. Life in America comes to a standstill. It is so eerie to go outside and look up at a sky devoid of aircraft and to switch TV channels and find nothing but somber talking heads. Erstwhile celebrities speechless as new heroes (New York firemen and police) replace them. Sports superstars shake in their shoes, for who cares about their scores or records now? The twenty Islamic terrorists are discussed everywhere.

It is a second Pearl Harbor—only worse, for this happens on live television. America's innocence and sense of invulnerability is gone forever. In the days that follow, the U. S. stock market remains closed and world markets reel.

Monday, September 17, Wall Street reopens. The Dow plunges 620 points. Two days later, the economy of the nation appears to be crumbling, the entire airline industry teetering on the edge of bankruptcy. Within a week, even foreign airlines cut staff by 25 percent. All around the world, people dependant on tourism for their livelihoods now fear the future, for America and Americans represent a staggering 70 percent of world tourism.

Thursday, September 20, the stock market plummets 380 more points. That evening, the president addresses Congress (strangely united for a change). It is a deeply sobering speech, for no one knows what is coming next . . . The following day, Friday the twenty-first, it is announced that this week represents the greatest weekly drop of the Dow since 1933, in one of the darkest weeks of the Great Depression.

About that time, Stella had written these words in her journal:

> People think I'm crazy for not canceling my trip to Greece
> and Turkey. There's such paranoia about ever traveling again,
> especially in an airplane. But I've made it a matter of prayer,
> and I'm convinced it is God's will that I should go. After all,
> He is still in control of this universe.

Stella had also been forced to articulate, at least to herself, why the cruise was so important to her:

> I guess it's because I need to get away, away from memories

of Bob. I need to decide what I'm going to do with the rest of my life. Since his passing, my life has been in a free fall. So has my writing. Furthermore, I just can't seem to get rid of the dark cloud that has hovered over me for almost twenty-three long years. Closure—how I long for closure! Perhaps new insights will come to me on the Mediterranean. Perhaps I'll find solace and resolution, though I can't really see how.

Suddenly, outside her window a sight appears that she'd seen only in dreams: the long peninsula of Italy. And then the blue of the Great Sea, and the plane begins the long descent to Athens. *Athens!*

ATHENS

Petros, the Greek driver, is waiting by the big Mercedes bus. Led by Dily, the jolly British tour guide, Stella and the other arrivals board. About a quarter of the Americans who signed on fail to appear. It could have been worse: other tour directors are forced to cancel the rest of that tourist season.

After taking a brief nap in her room at the centrally located Caravel Hotel, Stella descends to the lobby and begins to get acquainted with her fellow tour mates. She'd deliberately planned for this cruise to be a solo experience, but now, in this strange city and strange country, she isn't so sure that it had been a wise decision.

Outside, by the waiting bus, other travel partners begin to join her. *Oh my! Couple after couple. Am I ever going to be a misfit! Hadn't thought of that . . . Oh oh! Only one other person traveling alone. Not him! He's clearly on the prowl. Oh, dear God, will I be forced to sit with him by default?*

At the last possible moment, a beautiful young woman with long naturally blonde hair descends the steps toward the bus. Her step is fluid and she wears sensible shoes, made-to-look-worn-before-they-were-bought jeans, and a T-shirt of muted blue. Her eyes are bright with a look of isn't-this-a-wonderful-world? No makeup is needed or wanted. *Here might be my salvation!* Cutting off the raptor with the predatory eyes, she swiftly intercepts the newest arrival and introduces herself: "Hi! I'm Stella Andersen from Denver, and it appears there aren't many non-couples on this tour."

The blonde dimples. "Isn't that the truth! Ever since I saw the tour roster, I've been wondering if I was wise to travel alone. Oh, I almost forgot; I'm Melissa Williams from Santa Barbara," and almost in a whisper, "if you'll save me from that guy over there, I'll be eternally grateful!"

And so ends Stella's aloneness almost before it begins. They take a front seat so they won't miss anything. Melissa rummages in her canvas messenger bag for sunglasses. Petros is unbelievable: hogging the middle of the narrow streets, barreling through spaces you'd never believe a car could get through, much less a bus, not slowing a second for motorcyclists, who scatter like schools of fish.

Along the way, the two women get better acquainted.

"Well, I'll be first," volunteers Melissa, in her low but musical voice. "I just graduated from college with an English major. My folks gave me this tour as a graduation gift. They told me to pick any cruise I wanted—though, once I chose, they seemed terribly afraid that, over here, some Greek or Turk might abduct me."

Stella laughs and says, "I'm not sure that I blame your folks. They did take a bit of a risk."

Melissa says, "You're kind. What about you?"

"Me? Well, I'm from the Rockies—Conifer, to be exact, forty miles west of Denver. I was an air force wife until almost two years ago when my husband, Bob, died from a stroke."

"Oh, I'm sorry. Did he have any advance warnings?"

"Not really, except that he had high blood pressure—and a high-pressure job: base commander. He never learned how to relax, and he hated to take vacations. He was certain that everything would collapse the moment he left."

"And you—did you take vacations?"

"Without him? Not long ones. I'd just do occasional visits with family. Sometimes Bob came along, but it was as if he was always double-parked."

"Do you have any children?"

"No," with a sigh. "We never had any."

"Oh, sorry."

"You needn't be. How I wish there *were* children, but Bob was—er—I mean, we weren't able to have any."

The next morning, after boarding the bus and sitting down, Melissa leans forward and says, in a low voice, "You missed a rather ugly scene. You-know-who tried to take the seat I saved for you. *Demanded* it, in fact. When I said no, he got angry and snarled his way down the aisle."

"Hm. I don't like the looks of this."

"Neither do I. Oh, I'm sorry I brought him up on such a

beautiful morning in this legendary city. I hope to learn more about the Greek culture and history—one of my favorite subjects in school. How about you: do you know much about Greece?"

"Just a little. Apparently a lot of things happened here first, such as democracy for starters—long before ours! And I've always been impressed by how timeless—even contemporary—their art appears."

"True," muses Melissa. "Even today we idealize men and women who resemble those ancient Greek statues."

"And then there's drama," continues Stella, "which in turn brings up psychology—"

"But of course!" breaks in Melissa, "Who could define an *Oedipus Complex* without Oedipus?"

Stella smiles, then adds, as a sort of afterthought: "Even sports began here with the Olympics."

"Speaking of the Olympics," breaks in Melissa, "look out the window. We're pulling into the stadium where the Olympics were reborn—in 1896, I believe it was. Let's see, where's my camera?"

Before getting off the bus at the next spot, Dily comes on the microphone: "Listen, my little ducklings, we just arrived at the *Acropolis,* the Greek term for the highest elevation in a town. We are about to see some of the world's oldest surviving buildings. The Parthenon was built between 447 and 438 BC, the Propylaia between 437 and 432, the Temple of Athena Nike between 432 and 431, and the Erechtheion between 421 and 406."

"And we think our U. S. buildings are old!" chuckles Melissa.

"This incredible building program was coordinated by

Pericles, one of Athens's greatest leaders, who ruled between 461 and 429 BC His was the Golden Age of the city; not until the Renaissance—more than a millennium and a half later—would the Western World see such another flowering of the arts."

"Alexander the Great respected the city, as did his successors. Then came Rome. But here the conquered, conquered the conqueror. Under the Emperor Hadrian and his successors the culture of Greece superseded that of Rome. It was an interesting marriage: Rome's military might brought relative peace, and its architectural genius provided roads, bridges, baths, and aqueducts, many of which survive to this day. But the arenas of the mind and the arts—ah! That was all Greek."

"Pontificates just like my professor back home," interjects Melissa in a whisper.

"Then Athens went into a long decline. The Byzantines brought with them Orthodox Christianity and closed the great pagan temples. In 1457, three years after the fall of Constantinople, Mehmet II captured Athens, and it remained in Turkish hands until the nineteenth century. The Parthenon then became a mosque."

"But the greatest tragedy of all came from the Venetians. During one of their wars with the Ottoman Empire, in 1487, a Venetian soldier committed one of the most barbaric acts in recorded history: he tossed a grenade into the midst of the Parthenon that had lasted for two thousand years, and all but wrecked it. It has never been the same since. By the way, if any of you wish to see what it looked like *before* the grenade, there is an exact replica (only complete) in Nashville, Tennessee."

"I've seen the replica," notes Stella. "It's amazing."

"But in spite of the grenade, what is left is monumental

enough. If you want to see the original frieze, it's in the British Museum and called "Elgin's Marbles," after the Brit that saved—or stole—them, depending on whether you are British or Greek.

"You are about to experience a mob, as you will be sharing the Acropolis with tourists from around the world. They come here by the millions to see the almost mythical Parthenon at least once before they die."

"Now, let's leave the bus, but *stay together!* And experience the greatest babble of foreign tongues you will ever hear in your lifetime."

Late that evening, the two women gather in Stella's room to compare notes. After they settle down in soft chairs, Stella breaks the silence:

"What a day! I've a severe case of information overload," she says, kicking off her shoes.

"Isn't *that* the truth? I don't know just what I expected to see, but frankly, I'm overwhelmed. I saw and heard so much that it'll take a long time to digest it all."

"True indeed. But what stands out the most?"

There's a long silence during which Melissa runs her fingers through her long hair as though they were doing the searching. Finally, she says just two words: "Mars Hill."

"Bingo! I agree. But it wasn't what Mama Duck said, was it?"

"No indeed. It came from the stragglers to our group—the two men who flew in from London last night. They were delayed because SwissAir just filed for bankruptcy. I don't remember their names, but they're both really good looking."

"So you noticed too."

"It was hard not to. And remember how they came to our rescue?"

"That *was* kind of funny, Stella. As we were nearing the base of the Parthenon, he—"

"His name's Karl, isn't it?"

"Yep. Well, Karl deliberately ran into me, and there was no need for it. Then several steps later, he did it again, only this time it bordered on something more intimate. I stopped and said, 'Cut it out, Karl!' Instead of getting the message, he leered at me and said, 'You're fair game to any man who's got the guts to . . . ' At this very moment, a strong hand—backed up by broad muscular shoulders—clasped Karl's shoulder, and a deep voice rumbled, 'You heard the lady, Karl. Now *back off!* We'll have no more of this!'"

"And I noticed he did just *that.* I tried to catch the eye of the SwissAir The Younger, but he and the older man—wonder if they're father and son?—moved on. But I noticed that the two men were never very far away from us after that."

"But you said 'Mars Hill.'"

"Oh, I'm coming to that. But first, did you, by any chance, bring a Bible along?"

"Of course! Let me get it. Here it is! Acts 17, wasn't it?"

"Yes. It has to do with the apostle Paul's speech to the Athenians on Mars Hill."

"Correct. AD 60, I believe the guide said."

"Well, as a literature major, I really delved into Greek mythology. So when Dily led us to the north part of the Acropolis, to the Hill of Ares, where justice was rendered in Mycenaean times—"

Stella breaks in: "Oh yes! Just to think that it was on that very hill that the fleeing Orestes had to account for murdering his mother."

"True, but more importantly—to Christians at least—was what Paul said there. I couldn't believe it when SwissAir The Elder climbed to the top of the hill, and by *memory* recited the speech in its entirety. Read it, Stella!"

"OK. Here it is, beginning with verse 22:

Then Paul stood in the midst of Mars' hill, and said, Ye men of Athens, I perceive that in all things ye are too superstitious. For as I passed by, and beheld your devotions, I found an altar with this inscription, TO THE UNKNOWN GOD. Whom therefore ye ignorantly worship, him declare I unto you. God that made the world and all things therein, seeing that he is Lord of heaven and earth, dwelleth not in temples made with hands; Neither is worshipped with men's hands, as though he needed any thing, seeing he giveth to all life, and breath, and all things; And hath made of one blood all nations of men for to dwell on all the face of the earth, and hath determined the times before appointed, and the bounds of their habitation; That they should seek the Lord, if haply they might feel after him, and find him, though he be not far from every one of us: For in him we live, and move, and have our being; as certain also of your own poets have said. For we are also his offspring. Forasmuch then as we are the offspring of God, we ought not to think that the Godhead is like unto gold, or silver, or stone, graven by art and man's device. And the times of this ignorance God winked at; but now commandeth all men every where to repent: Because he hath appointed a day, in the which he will judge the world in righteousness by *that* man whom he hath ordained; *whereof* he hath given assurance unto all *men*, in that he hath raised him from the dead. (Acts 17:22–31 KJV)

"Oh Stella, what a speaker that man is! When he concluded, there was applause coming from all over the Acropolis. I even saw Hindus and Muslims clapping! A preacher couldn't have done it better."

"Who knows? Maybe he *is* one."

"Huh-uh. He doesn't dress or act like one. And he laughs too much."

"So preachers aren't supposed to laugh?"

"Oh, you know what I mean. He just doesn't seem the type."

"Perhaps not. But you still haven't *really* answered my question. I'm most interested in just what it was that made Mars Hill the high-point of the day for you."

After a long pause, very haltingly, Melissa answers. "Oh, I don't know, Stella. In fact, I've only known you one day—yet, somehow I feel I've known you *much longer*."

"I feel the same way about you. But go on . . . "

"Well, I guess I need to share with you some of my childhood and growing-up years, in order for this to make much sense."

"I'd be honored."

"First of all, and don't get me wrong—I *love* Dad and Mom. They'd give everything they own—which is a lot—for me. It's just that neither of them know God as that man on Mars Hill did this morning! Theirs is such a . . . uh, perfunctory religion. You know, Easter and Christmas people with not much in between.

"So how did *you* find the Lord, if not from them?"

"That's a long story. But, in short, I had a teacher who really knew God. I was a third-grader at the time, and my folks had enrolled me in an upscale parochial school . . . so I'd get my ethics and morals from a proper source, I guess. Well, day by day, in this man's class, more by what he *was* than what he *said*, I came to know God and to love Him. And God has been with me every step of the way since then—even in . . . in . . ."

"In *what?*"

"Me and my big mouth! I can't believe I'm telling you this—almost a complete stranger."

"I hope not for long."

"Well, it has to do with a man—*another* man, who came into my life. I've always received more attention than was good for me. Sometimes I feel beauty can be a curse. You ought to know, because you're beautiful—I've seen men staring at you. At any rate, I'd just been chosen Rose Bowl Queen."

"You don't say! What an honor!"

"True, it *was* an honor, and I'm afraid I let it go to my head. I was besieged by men who wanted to take me out. But it wasn't just the taking out—"

"I know, I know. They wanted more than just a date."

"Yes. More—*much* more! And I really fell for one of them." Melissa fingers the two-toned antique watch on her wrist. "He was a fairy tale prince who swept me off my feet. He had it all: looks, charisma, wit, money. I never knew which car he'd pick me up in—Bentley, Ferrari, Rolls, Lamborghini. He took me to the most expensive restaurants and gave me lavish gifts. But there was an expected price tag."

"Of course! With that type, there usually is. Did you meet his parents?"

"His mother, yes. She is a thrice-divorced socialite. His father lives in Europe, shuttling from chateau to chateau. Well, he wanted to fly me to Majorca for a weekend, but I said no. He couldn't understand it. His face darkened, and he snarled, 'Surely such a beauty queen as you can't be *that* lily white and prudish! You certainly aren't a *virgin* are you?' He said it like it was an obscene word."

"So what did you tell him?"

"I admitted that I was."

"And what happened?"

"He got up from the table and disappeared. About five minutes later, the maitre d' came over to my table and announced that a taxi was waiting for me outside."

"Just like that?"

"Just like that—and I haven't seen him since. And sometimes I've wondered . . ."

"Wondered what?"

"Whether or not I was stupidly naive. After all, nobody waits these days."

"I admire you, dear, for having such self-respect."

"Oh, Stella, it was more than that. Long ago, I vowed that on my wedding night, I'll present my husband with the ultimate gift within my power—virginity. And my hope against hope is that he'll have the same gift for me. I vowed it to God. But oh, Stella, it's been a *hard vow to keep*! I've felt so alone. Yet, having said that, I'm still glad I found out now rather than later, when I'd given my heart to him," she says, breaking down.

Stella takes her into her arms and just holds her for a very long time. It is after midnight when, after praying with Melissa, she finally returns to her room.

STEPPING BACK IN TIME

The next morning, Stella wakes early and completes her morning ritual of recording thoughts in her journal. She stretches and lingers for a few moments between the luxurious sheets. After showering, she retrieves her miniature hair dryer and dries her casual hair style in five minutes flat. It doesn't take long to pick out something from the suitcase. Linen seems a good choice for the day. She applies moisturizer. No makeup is wanted or needed. After zipping up the case, she heads down to breakfast and the tour bus.

To the casual observer, the relationship between the two women remains unchanged. But that is merely an illusion for there is now a deep bond between them—the bond born in that crucible of tears.

The travelers are quiet on this third day, no one saying much, just looking. At the Corinth Canal they dutifully get out, walk across the bridge, look down at the ship far below, take in the guide's monotone commentary, and return to the bus.

Then they come to the citadel of the Mycenaean kings. Stella and Melissa leave the bus with high hopes, but Dily (by now, everyone calls her "Mama Duck") apparently drained her historical reservoirs in Athens; so she leaves them to drift about aimlessly, like so many wandering sheep. Just ahead, near an impressive gateway, they see a gathering crowd. And the center of attention is the speaker of Mars Hill. People from all over, not just from their tour group, are feverishly taking notes. Stella and Melissa whip out their pens and notebooks and prepare to do likewise.

"You are seeing this morning one of the greatest sights of

the ancient world: the Lion Gate. Notice the regal lions on either side, and especially the flat slab at the top of the doorway—this was long before the Romans invented the arch. The story of the founding of this hilltop palace-citadel is shrouded in the mists of myth. But tradition has it that it was founded by Perseus, son of Zeus and Danae, and that he used the mythical Cyclopes to haul in and position these great stones."

There is magic in his voice: one moment they're standing a short distance from their air-conditioned Mercedes bus, and another moment, they're whirled backwards to another time, another age. He takes them farther back than even David and Solomon—almost as far back as Moses and the Exodus—twelve hundred and fifty years before Christ.

These are not merely cobwebby history lectures, either, but rather stories of bygone, flesh-and-blood-real people. They ride by, attired in the richest fabrics, and their horses snort and paw their hooves on the stony streets in their impatience to be on their way to Athens, or perhaps to Troy.

Late that afternoon, the tour reaches the Athenian seaport of Piraeus. There at the dock is a sleek ship, Royal Olympic's *Stella Solaris.* After finding their rooms on board, the two women meet on the top deck to watch the ship's sunset departure from the harbor. After the Greek coastline with its myriad of flickering lights fades from view, they sit down in the beautiful dining hall for dinner. Afterwards they're too tired to talk, so they turn in early.

Stella pulls on her favorite pajamas with the white clouds.

Almost as soon as her head hits the pillow, she's dreaming of gods and goddesses, kings and queens, Helen and the thousand ships she launched.

ISTANBUL

Dawn welcomes a rest day at sea. Not long after breakfast, Melissa tracks down Stella, who is ensconced in a deck chair, pad and pen in lap, staring vacantly out to sea.

"I thought I'd find you here."

Stella awakens from her trance and smiles. "Sit down. My, it's good to see you! For a moment, I thought you were Helen of Troy."

"Silly," the vision smiles and looks down, "Helen didn't wear jeans." Then with quicksilver swiftness she adds, "Now what is Madame thinking about this glorious morning?"

"Yesterday."

"Me too. I didn't see how one day could impact me more than the day in Athens, but yesterday did."

"No small thanks to the bard of Mars Hill."

"Oh Stella! I found out their names. Yes, I'll admit it: I snooped."

"You *didn't*!"

"I did. Mars Hill is John N. Winters, Ph.D. times two."

"*Two?*"

"Correct. One Ph.D. in history, and one in religion. He's a college professor."

"Could've known that . . . and the son?"

"Surely you didn't expect me to be brazen enough to look him up too, did you?"

"I most surely *did.* Come on, 'fess up."

"Well," smiling demurely, "if you *must* know—his name is Joseph, but I may call him Joe."

"Oh? It's gone as far as that, has it?"

"Y-e-s. Dr. John asked if they might sit at my table at breakfast, and I said they could. Joseph—Joe—just asked with his eyes. I like his eyes."

"So I see. And what does the young man do?"

"He's a park ranger. In Grand Canyon National Park—on the North Rim."

"What a place to live!"

"That's what I told him. He said I should visit it."

"And you answered?"

"I said, 'I might just do that—some day.'"

Stella laughs, "Well, now we finally know who they are," and she looks again out at the deep blue of the Mediterranean.

"Come now, Stella, there's a faraway look in your eyes this morning that wasn't there two days ago. I'll bet it has to do with yesterday."

Silence. Finally, "Well, yes, it does. It has to do with . . . er . . . Dr. John, as you call him, and his ability to make the past come alive. When we got off the bus, it was just a warm October day and piles of shaped rocks on top of a hill."

"And afterwards?"

"Well, afterwards . . . let's see. It was story after story. It was King Atreus of Mycenae and that grisly meal."

"Ugh! Just the mere thought of such a diabolical thing! After having served a delicious banquet, genially informing his brother Thyestes that he had just eaten his own sons!"

"True, but it wasn't just that ghastly deed that made such

an impression on me. And it wasn't just the fact that we saw the great drama of famed Greek playwright Aeschylus performed live before our eyes, but there by the Lion Gate we saw Agamemnon, son of Atreus, ride down the cobbled street with his warriors on their way to Troy to help his brother Menelaus of Sparta recapture his wife, Helen of Troy—"

"Oh, Stella, wasn't it eerie? Just think, Agamemnon of Homer's *Illiad* left that citadel we walked across and explored, bidding good-bye to his lovely queen and sister of Helen, Clytemnestra —I hadn't known *that* before. Then ten years later, he returns through that same Lion Gate, the conqueror of Troy, with shouts of triumph greeting his arrival, only to be murdered by the queen and a surviving son of Thyestes inside the palace up the hill. And then—oh my! to be, in turn, killed by her own son and daughter on that very spot eight years later."

"Yes . . . but it was far more than just gore, the way Dr. Winters told the story. It was the effect of breaking God's Law . . . how did he put it? Oh yes, here it is in my notes: 'It matters not whether you believe in the existence of such universal law, it is built into the very fabric of the universe: as we do unto others will sooner or later circle around and be done unto us and our descendants. The Golden Rule—or the Corroded Rule—the results depend on our acts.'"

"Oh Stella, I don't know about you, but I'd never realized before yesterday that Homer—old, feeble, and blind—undoubtedly walked through that Lion Gate any number of times and right there on that hill, and also in other great cities all across Greece, recited—or sang *by memory* all twenty hours of *The Illiad* and *The Odyssey*! Had not Dr. Winters taken us with him on yesterday's journey into the past, it would never have become so real to us. *Never!*"

"True indeed, Melissa. It was all the more real to me since I've actually seen *Oresteia* performed live by great actors, but somehow, separated from its setting, it didn't seem quite real. Yesterday, as he was talking, in my mind's eye I could see those long ago stage characters, only now they were performing on their *real* stage. Oh yes, and for the first time, the siege of Troy seems real, and with real people."

"And Helen of Troy, perhaps the most beautiful woman since Eve—yet what tragedy followed her every step. I just can't get those women out of my head. Isn't it true that beauty can be a curse?"

"Yes. Or it can be a blessing . . . though, come to think about it, there weren't many female blessings in the stories he told yesterday."

"He looks at you—often, you know, when he thinks nobody's watching."

"Oh come now, Melissa! You're just a romantic who imagines things."

"Oh? And I just 'imagine' that you do the same?"

"Come on, I'm not on the witness stand. Let's talk about something else. Let's continue on from two days ago."

"In what way, Stella?"

"Well, I'm interested in finding out more about your journey. What happened between the third-grader and the Rose Bowl Queen?"

"That's a long story."

"What else do we have to do?"

"OK. Well, I grew up doted on. Dad was a real estate

developer and made lots of money. Mom stayed home. Change that: Mom was and is a socialite. She lives for society. I had a nanny, of course. A string of them. I grew up living in books—our house was full of them, and most of my friends were between their covers."

"Goodness, Melissa, it sounds like you were lonely."

"I was. Am."

"Why?"

"Oh, a combination of my love for God, our social status in the community, my love for books . . ."

"And your beauty?"

"Oh yes, *that*. That was and *is* a two-edged sword. You ought to know."

"So you attended college in California?"

"Yes, that's where I came in that first night."

"I know. But forgive me for wanting more than that. What's behind those starry eyes of yours? What is it that you want to do with the rest of your life?"

"You'll laugh."

"I won't either. Just try me!"

"Well, it sounds so ridiculously old-fashioned, I hate to even admit it."

"*Please?*"

"Oh, all right! I just want to marry a wonderful Christian man that I admire and adore."

"And?"

"And," blushing scarlet, "have his children. I *love* children. Always have. I want to be a full-time housewife and mother. I want to homeschool them as long as possible before they go on to advanced study . . . I want to be the mom I never had."

"I know. I feel that way too."

"What do you mean?"

"Well, since we—uh—don't have any children of our own, I've mothered as many children as my husband let me."

"And now that he's gone?"

"Oh, I've been treading water. I don't know what God wants me to do with the rest of my life . . . besides writing, of course. As an air force wife, most of my decisions were made for me. Bob was the commander, and I, regrettably, was the private. So I obeyed for over twenty years."

"And now?"

"Well, now I feel like this incredible load has been lifted from my shoulders. I get to actually make decisions on my own. It's both exhilarating and scary."

"I know, Stella, I know. Now that I've graduated, I don't know what to do or where to go. I just know I don't want to go back to that empty house."

"And?"

"Oh, I just want to keep growing, keep learning. Life without it would be dead-end. I'd like to travel a lot (think of how much deeper thinkers we are about life and our acts than was true two days ago!), help people wherever the need is greatest. Help out in my church. Perhaps even write like you . . . oh look! We're coming into the Dardanelles!"

"And then . . . the great Sea of Marmara."

"And then—Istanbul!" completes Melissa.

"Would you ladies care to join us?" asks John Winters, standing. "We've commandeered four deck chairs because it's going to get pretty crowded here at the bow as we approach the Golden Horn."

"Why, thank you!" says Stella. "Is that all right with you, Melissa?"

"Why sure," glancing hesitantly at Joe.

"Good! Make yourselves at home, and get comfortable."

Somewhat awkward moments follow. Finally, Melissa, seeking to get a conversation going, turns to the professor and says, "Dr. John—I mean Winters—"

He smiles and says, "Dr. John is fine. I like it coming from you."

"Well, all right," clearly ill at ease at this slip of the tongue. "I have a favor to ask of you."

"Your wish is my command."

"Oh, it's not a command. It's just that, earlier today, Stella and I were debriefing about yesterday—"

He breaks in again and says, "Are you *sure* you two aren't mother and daughter? Same natural blonde hair, same features—same mannerisms!"

"Sorry to disappoint you, Dr. Winters, but we'd never met before we arrived in Athens," says Stella.

"Well, Joe and I just couldn't help wondering. But I'm sorry for interrupting. Tell us more about your—uh—'debriefing,' as you put it."

Melissa, even more flustered now, says, "We were just discussing Mycenae and the incredible difference your unannounced lecture made."

He laughs. "I'm not sure Mama Duck was that pleased, but I just decided to whip out some notes, and pretend I was surrounded by students, and try to make the place real to them. Clearly, Dily didn't have anything planned for us."

"That's just it! We were stumbling around, not having the faintest idea of what it was we were approaching. Then you told us stories, and suddenly, the whole hilltop came alive. The entire tragedy. The Trojan War. *The Oresteia*. Life itself. What a difference your words made!"

"I agree," adds Stella. "I came on this cruise in order to learn, to grow, and I feel short-changed when a day passes without such growth."

"Well thank you, both of you. I didn't know if I was being presumptuous by requisitioning the Lion Gate."

"It most certainly wasn't, Dad," interjects Joe. "You live and breathe this stuff. It's almost a college education just to travel with you."

"All three of you flatter me. But it all started with your wanting a favor. What was it, Miss—?"

"Melissa's fine, Dr. John. Just consider me as another of your students. But to answer your question, up ahead an hour or so is another of this world's greatest cities. And I know so little about it, except for that old song, 'Is-tan-bul— Con-stan-tinople.'"

Laughter.

"The favor I ask of you—and I realize it's a *big* one—is this: would you mind telling us about the history, lore, and magic of the city ahead?"

"Not at all," looking from face to face. "Sure it won't bore you?"

"Try us!" comes in triplicate.

"Very well. You guys chat a bit while I walk down the deck a ways and gather my thoughts."

"I'm ready, if you are—I see you're taking notes. Good idea. It helps to reinforce what is said. Stop me anywhere along the way where you have questions, or where I haven't been clear."

Heads nod.

"Well, on the site where Europe and Asia meet, a town was born back—oh, around 700 BC. It was called Byzantium. A thousand years later, the Emperor Constantine came to the throne."

"Wasn't he the first Christian emperor of Rome?"

"Yes . . . and no. His mother, Helena, became a Christian. His father, General Constantias, was most definitely not. Upon his father's death, his troops anointed the son Caesar. With six generals all claiming to be Caesar at once, war raged for seventeen long years. In 312, Constantine had a dream in which he saw a flaming cross in the sky, along with three Greek words, *en toutoi nika* (in this sign conquer). When he awoke the next morning, he ordered the creation of a new standard to be carried in the forefront of the battle that day. That standard, carrying the initials of Christ interwoven with a cross, became known as the *labarium*. From that time on, his soldiers were victorious in every battle.

"When he finally became master of the vast Roman World, Constantine was faced with a great decision: should he rule in Rome, as previous emperors had done? He finally concluded that Rome was too dissolute to be used as his seat of government. But Byzantium was at the heart of Christianity's Seven Churches. So he made the far-reaching decision to move the imperial capital there.

"In November of 324, Constantine the Great led a small army of aides, engineers, architects, priests, and the like from the harbor of Byzantium out across the nearby hills. As they progressed, the foundation positions of the proposed new capital were marked. Afterwards, he summoned thousands of workmen to build the great city. And the finest and most acclaimed art in the Empire was requisitioned along with Christian relics, which his mother, Helena, supervised.

"Massive walls forty miles long and up to 200 feet thick were constructed. Inside, they built palaces, homes, administrative buildings, squares, boulevards, and fountains, as well as a magnificent hippodrome, seating 70,000 people. The city was dedicated on May 11, 330. Within seven years, 50,000 people had moved in; by 400, the population grew to 100,000; and by 500, it was almost a million, which was staggering for a walled city! For over a thousand years it would remain the richest, most beautiful, and most civilized city in the world. In the emperor's honor, the city was called 'Constantinople.'"

"My, how can you remember all this?" asks the amazed Melissa.

"I guess I should have told you: I lecture on these ancient cities all the time at the university."

"Oh, in that case I'm much less impressed," Melissa retorts with an impish grin, and they all break into laughter.

By this time, as had been true the day before at Mycenae, a crowd of fellow travelers is gathering around him.

"Constantine lived only thirteen more years. At Easter of 337, there was an empirewide celebration of his reign. But he knew the sands of his life were running out. As the end drew near, he finally took the long-delayed step: he called for a priest to administer the sacrament of baptism to him. He had many sins to account for, including the executions of a wife, son, and nephew. But even so, he was a far better man than most rulers of his time."

"I'm curious," says a distinguished-looking man in the crowd. "I'm a scientist, not a historian, and am rather ashamed to admit how ignorant I am about this bygone world you describe. My head is spinning, in fact. I *do* know that much of this part of the world is Muslim rather than Christian—how did the change take place?"

"I'm glad you asked that question, sir, as I was about to end the lecture here, not wanting to tire you."

From all sides come voices saying, "Go on!" "Please continue!" "Don't stop now!"

"Very well. As I said, Constantinople, the New Rome, became the greatest city in the world. Because of Byzantium, the entire empire was renamed, becoming the Byzantine Empire. As the Vandals attacked again and again, ancient Rome became little more than a ghost town. Do any of you remember the name of the greatest Byzantine emperor?"

"Wasn't it Justinian?" asks Stella.

"Correct!" looking at her with new respect. "Now I'll *really* be impressed if you know the name of the beautiful courtesan who became his empress."

"Theodora," she blurts out, as she stealthily shoves her tourist book, *Constantinople: Obscure Facts to Dazzle and Impress*, back into her jacket pocket.

"Right again! Maybe *you* should be giving this lecture. At any rate, under Justinian's great general Belisarius, the empire was vastly expanded: all of North Africa recaptured from the Vandals, and its legal system—"

"I know, I know!" responds a young man in the crowd. I studied it in law school. Wasn't it called the Code of Justinian?"

"Correct. It lasted for almost a thousand years, and lives on in modern jurisprudence. Moving on, Justinian was also responsible for the construction of one of the most beautiful buildings ever built, the *Hagia Sophia.* Ten thousand workers were requisitioned, and it cost an astronomical $134 million, which just about broke the imperial treasury. On December 26, 537, the emperor and patriarch of Constantinople led the inaugural procession into the great cathedral. Filled with awe and joy, Justinian lifted his hands and cried out, 'Glory be to God who has thought me worthy to accomplish so great a work! O Solomon, I have vanquished you!'"

"Now there's an ego for you!" mutters Joe.

"After Justinian, the vast empire began to contract. Early in the eighth century, the emperor, Leo III, became concerned about the explosion of iconography—artistic representations of Christ, the virgin Mary, and the saints. Fearing they were bringing paganism back, he ordered them to be destroyed and for church murals to be covered with plaster. The edict was greeted with empirewide rage. In the end, the pope withdrew the papacy from the empire over the issue. Thereafter, the bishop of Rome ruled the churches of the West and the patriarchs of Constantinople ruled the churches of the East. That historic schism continues to this very day.

"Now let's step back to the year 570, when a man named Mohammed was born into a poor desert family. This unlettered child would grow up to write one of the world's most significant books, the Koran. Since he was a descendant of Abraham and

Hagar, Mohammed felt himself to be heir to both Jewish and Christian traditions and thought. Both were incorporated into the Koran. The new faith spread like fire in a tinder-dry forest. The Arabians, led by great tacticians and mounted on some of the world's fastest horses, then set out to conquer the Mediterranean world. Saracen fleets attacked by sea as horsemen attacked by land. 'There is no God but Allah, and Mohammed is his prophet!' rang out everywhere, and cities that had been Christian since apostolic times now turned Muslim. Almost overnight the great Christian East became the great Muslim East, and the Mediterranean became an Arab lake.

"During the Crusades, hundreds of thousands of Christians headed to the Holy Land to wrest control from the Arabs. The eight Crusades failed. But they did attack their Christian host city, Constantinople, in 1202 and sacked it. The Byzantine Empire never fully recovered. Even today the East has never forgiven the West for that violation. Almost unbelievably, however, Constantinople lasted until May 29, 1453, when it at last fell to the Ottoman Turks.

"The Turks turned the *Hagia Sophia* into a mosque, and attached minarets. They would rule until the twentieth century, gradually becoming weaker as centuries passed. But that great city, renamed Istanbul, continued to thrive, and today there are some 17 million people living in its vicinity.

"Wait until you see it. Just as is true with Athens, it is almost unthinkable not to see it before one dies!

"I thank you."

Sustained applause from the surrounding crowd. Many additional questions are asked. Only as the ship approaches the legendary city does everyone turn to face . . . Istanbul.

That night at the caravanserai, Dr. John and Joe escort Stella and Melissa to dinner. Afterwards the lovely Turkish dancers entrance their audience.

And no one wants to be far from Dr. John the next day as they tour the city. Inside the *Hagia Sophia* with magnificent central columns said to have been plundered from Ephesus, the third greatest city of its time, Stella and Melissa look up and up into the great dome. Almost a millennium and a half have passed, yet it still staggers the viewer. Then on to the famous Blue Mosque with its six minarets, the Topkapi Palace, and concluding with carpet shops.

Then at sunset, as the minaret and dome-silhouetted saffron sky gradually turns dark, the *Stella Solaris* sails out of the Golden Horn. On deck there is only an awed silence.

That night in Melissa's stateroom, the two women relive the last two days.

"He's not married," announces Melissa out of the blue.

"I knew *that*," retorts Stella. "He's only twenty-six."

"I'm referring to Dr. John. His wife died six and a half years ago. Breast cancer. He's lonely."

"So how did you find all that out, you inquisitive woman?"

"Just asked Joe."

"You two seem to be getting along awfully well. Karl just glowers at you—oh if looks could kill, Joe'd be dead."

"So he does. He's kind of funny—in a scary way. I'd be

afraid of him without Joe to protect me. And Joe's a Christian, like his father. I could never marry a non-Christian."

"*So!* It's gone that far, has it?"

Melissa's face turns scarlet. "Of—of *course* not!" she answers. "We're just friends. Good friends."

"Uh-huh. So I noticed."

"Stella, come now, is it just my imagination, or does your heart sing when you're near Dr. John? Your face glows, and a dreamy look comes into your eyes. I think someone's got a crush on Dr. John!"

"Me-*lissa!*"

"Well, don't you?"

EPHESUS

The foursome walk the streets of ancient Ephesus together. It's so good to have a tour guide who can bring the city to life for them.

At one point, Stella muses out loud, "It's all kind of surreal. At any point, I almost expect to see the apostle Paul walking towards me."

"Yes!" echoes Melissa. "It's hard to believe that archeologists have been able to restore so much of this ancient city. What really stopped me in my tracks, though, was seeing the sign of the fish in mosaics. And then, only a short distance away, indications that there were houses of ill-repute there too."

"What I can't get over," says Joe, "are the ancient public latrines—men and women together. No toilet paper, just a channel of water running by to wash your hands in. No thank you!"

"Well, the city *was* just what its counterparts are today," concludes the professor meditatively—"good and bad, virtue and vice, beauty and ugliness, the spiritual and the demonic. We just have to choose what we take with us."

At Kusadasi, on the Turkish Riviera, that evening, they can't help noticing screaming headlines in Turkish and Greek, and horrific photographs. Afghanistan is being bombed by American forces. Like others, Stella struggles with the unanswered heartache of war. *What about the children? I guess I can't really escape all those horrible things that are happening in the other world out there. It's been so nice to get away from it all, to bury myself in the past. Unfortunately, when I get off this ship, that other world will claim me again. Oh, I don't want to go back!*

THE GREEK ISLES AND THE LAST NIGHT

As hard as they try to clutch the days, they evade their grasp and slip away one after another. They come to the lonely Isle of Patmos where the apostle John wrote Revelation during the Domitian Persecution. According to tradition, while the heavenly apocalyptic vision took place, the voice of God cracked the ceiling of the cave where John dwelt. Next comes Mykonos with its windy streets and starkly white windmills. And the famous island "ruler," Petros the Pelican waddles in and out of shops to exact tribute and pose for shutter bugging tourists. Then came Rhodes with its medieval walled city, once ruled by the legendary Grand Marshals of the Knights of St. John. What an experience to walk inside such a perfectly preserved medieval city! Crete is next—the birthplace of the great Minoan kingdom that once reigned over this part of the world.

And finally they visit Santorini, said to have been the site of the mythical Atlantis—so heartstoppingly beautiful with its multicolored buildings hugging steep hillsides.

At last it arrives—the last bittersweet night on the *Stella Solaris*. After dinner with John and Joe, the violins of a Moldavian couple sob and sing their way into listeners' memories, concluded by the grand finale of singers, dancers, and orchestra, followed by walks on the moonlit deck, two by two.

And then, in Stella's cabin for the last time, the weary women stretch out and remember.

"So what stands out the most in the last few days?" asks Melissa.

"Oh, what happened at Rhodes. I hadn't realized that this ship was so old. Nor had I realized that we are experiencing its swan song, its last voyage. I didn't know that until we were leaving the harbor. As the pilot boat disengaged, its horn blasted three times, the *Stella Solaris* answered with three deafening blasts. Then the pilot boat blasted one more time, and the *Stella Solaris* answered with one, long, almost endless blast . . . and Rhodes slowly receded from view.

"I gravitated to the stern of the ship, and there all alone was a man who appeared to be the captain. Slowly, I approached him, hesitating to intrude upon the moment. He appeared to be almost in a trance, watching the Camelot-like walls and towers of Rhodes recede, the wake driving a snow-white wedge between the soft-blue waters of late afternoon. Before he turned, he wiped his eyes and returned the handkerchief to his pocket.

"'Ah, Madame,' he greeted me, 'what can I do for you?'

"'Ah . . . you are the captain?'

"'Assuredly, madame—co-captain—but just for this voyage.'

"Seeing my puzzled look, he explained, 'I'm retired now, but I was a cabin boy on the very first voyage of the *Stella Solaris* back in 1947. Oh, she lived up to her name in those days: the brightest star in Greek shipping! I fell in love with her, for ships are like women—all beautiful, but some more beautiful than others. In fact, it is said that there are only three perfect shapes in the world: a ship's hull, a violin, and a beautiful woman.'

"'I didn't know the *Stella Solaris* was so old. Why that makes her over half a century old!'

"'Yes, Madame—very old for a sea-faring grand dame.'

"'Uh, Captain, I'm curious. What was the significance of that interchange of blasts with the pilot boat a few minutes ago: three and three, and one and one?'

"'Ah, Madame, that's why you caught me wiping tears from my eyes. It was farewell. You see, this is the last voyage of this, my second love. For fifty-four long years, pilot boats have been ushering her in and out of the ancient harbor of Rhodes. Aboard that boat was an old man: the pilot who escorted us in and out fifty-four years ago—he and I are the same age. He was the one who sounded the horn, and I was the one who answered the last good-bye from *Stella* . . . I've been weeping ever since.'

"'So how many years have you served on this ship?'

"'Thirty-seven. Twenty-five as captain—longer than any other. That's why they let me be co-captain for this last voyage. Ah, she has been my life, Madame. Beautiful to me always, she's almost as beautiful as my wife, Danae, whom I first saw almost fifty years ago, right here, aft. Her long raven hair was blowing in the wind. When she looked back at me and smiled, my heart stopped. Took me three years before she promised to be my shipmate for life. We were married on this ship, and we've spent every anniversary on board.'

"'Danae was here with me until just moments ago. She left me alone with my grief.'

"'Oh, and I intruded; I'm so sorry!'

"'No! No! Madame. I like talking about *Stella*. By the way, they call me Captain Nicholas—and you?'

"'Stella.'

"'No! Ah, Madame, you are beautiful like *Stella Solaris*. The ship will never sail again, but you will always carry her in your heart, will you not?'

"I could only nod. I literally could not speak a word. And then we parted."

"So . . . Stella, what does *Stella Solaris* mean?"

"*Stella* means 'bright star' and *Solaris* means 'sun-like in intensity'—in other words, fifty-four years ago the ship was considered to be the brightest star in the Greek galaxy of ships."

"Stella . . . bright star. That you are. On this last evening together, I feel reflective. How I wish I had a mother like you. Why, you and I are more than friends—we've become soul sisters. And I envy Joe. He has a father, a real father to commune with. My father takes care of my creature comforts but never ever opens up his heart, mind, and soul to me the way Joe's father does."

"You care a lot about Joe, don't you?

"Yes. More than I ever dreamed possible. He's asked if he may write to me. If he may come to see me. He . . . he . . . told me he knows it's premature to say he loves me, but his heart is stirring, and he wants to get to know me better. He even quoted Victor

Hugo, saying he wants to know my very soul." Her voice trails off and there is a moment of silence as both women are lost in reverie, daring only privately to acknowledge the hidden heart-cry of every woman—to be known and cherished at the soul level.

Finally, Melissa breaks the spell, her eyes moist: "And he prayed that God would lead our lives and that, if it be His will, someday our two lives might merge into one."

"Bless you, my child! I thoroughly approve of him."

"And the father?"

"I thoroughly approve of him too."

"*How* thoroughly?"

"Well, he's asked if I will write to him—and if he may come to visit me."

"And you said?"

"I said yes, and he kissed my hand like a European."

"Are you falling in love?"

"Love? . . . I'm not absolutely sure." Mischievously, "I know I have a strong case of 'like' so far. All I can say is that my defenses appear to be crumbling."

Melissa, looking at her watch, exclaims, "Goodness! It's after midnight; so that means it's October twelfth, and we dock in Piraeus at dawn. So, on this last night, somehow I feel impressed to share something I rarely share with anyone outside my immediate family. It may perhaps explain some of my rather guarded responses to questions you've asked.

"Please *do.*"

"Well . . . uh . . . neither Mom nor Dad are my biological parents. I was adopted."

"But they *love* you, don't they?"

"Y-e-s, in their own way. They take pride in the attention I get from the media, but that isn't the same as unconditional love. I hate to say it because it sounds disloyal, but sometimes I've wondered why they adopted me in the first place. I've also wondered—wondered *many* times!—about my birth mother. Why she let me go and whether she loved me . . . whether she still thinks of me . . . and, I guess, today being my twenty-third birthday, it carries me back to those early years."

"Well, happy birthday, my dear! And to think I have no present to give you!"

"Oh, I don't need a present. I just wanted you to know, that's all."

"October 12. Hmm. You were born in—what year?"

"1978."

"Where?"

"In California."

"Where?"

"The Napa Valley, in a town you've probably never heard of."

"Try me."

"In St. Helena—in what used to be called 'The Old Sanitarium.'"

In The Old Sanitarium. Stella's face turns ashen. "It can't be! It can't be! *Dear Lord, it can't be!*"

"What are you talking about? What's got into you?"

Stella crosses the room and leans against the window sill. Then she turns and faces Melissa with an enigmatic expression on her face. She says, in a voice that shakes a little, "Now, *I* have a story to tell *you.*"

"Go ahead. I'm listening."

"A long time ago, when I was seventeen, I fell in love with someone—a nineteen-year-old guy, who was as handsome as a Greek god."

"The one you married?"

"No. He asked me to marry him, and I said yes. Then, just as it happened to you, he asked me to go away with him for a weekend. After all, we loved each other and would soon be married anyhow. I held out for interminable hours. Finally, my folks being gone on a trip, he wore me down and I finally said yes."

"And?"

"I went. And not long after, I realized I was pregnant."

"And?"

"I told him, but he just looked at me coldly and spat out, 'How *could* you have been so stupid? Not to take precautions!' And walked out the door. I've never seen him since."

"Oh you poor soul! What then?"

"I was so embarrassed! I dreaded breaking the news to my folks. When I did, it almost broke their hearts. Since I didn't believe in abortion, my folks sent me off to stay with a great aunt in another state until the baby came. I cried myself to sleep every night for it seemed that my entire world had caved in on me—that God had deserted me."

"Oh, Stella!"

"Well, the baby came—and she was *beautiful!* I fell in love with her at once. But I had no skills to speak of. I was just starting college and had no money. Then one day the kind doctor who delivered my baby called and said that a visiting couple who had seen my baby in the hospital nursery wanted to know if they could possibly adopt her. They were apparently nice people, and *very* well-to-do."

"And?"

"What *could* I say? I had nothing to offer her. So I said for him to have them checked out. They checked out fine. So I said yes. But there was a provision they insisted I sign and have notarized: I would promise to *never* try to contact my child—*ever.*"

"And?"

"I signed it. They took her away, and I've always kept my word."

"Oh my!"

"Well, I completed my bachelors and masters degrees. I became a teacher and a writer. I married and the years stumbled by . . . but oh! Inside my broken heart is my beautiful daughter—my daughter that I'd never see again! Every birthday, I imagine what she looks like, how she's grown. Has she grown up to love God? Does she wonder about me as I wonder about *her*? There's an empty space inside me that's bigger than Carlsbad Caverns! I used to think that, as the years passed and I got older, the anguish would go away.

"Has it?"

"No! A thousand times no! It only gets worse. It even affected my marriage. Bob couldn't understand it at all. He said once, 'Stella, she's dead to you forever—so *just forget about it!* I'm tired of seeing you weepy all the time.'"

"Not exactly empathetic, your Bob."

"So I kept it bottled up inside . . . until he died. Since that time, it's been worse than ever. My child should be a grown woman now. Finally, I laid the matter before my Lord, and I asked Him to guide my faltering footsteps, to show me what I should do with the rest of my life."

"And?"

"He impressed me to return to my writing . . . and get away, get *far* away from everything. Hence this cruise."

"Did you pray about that too?"

"Oh yes! *Especially* after September 11. But I had this overwhelming conviction that I should come. It couldn't have been a clearer mandate if God had told me aloud to go."

"And . . . you still feel the same now that you're here?"

"Yes. Oh yes! *Yes!*"

"By the way, I'm curious. How many years ago was your child born?"

"Twenty-three."

"What a coincidence!"

"Yes, isn't it?"

"I hope you don't mind, but you've got my curiosity up . . . . On what—"

"Oh don't. *Don't ask it!*"

Puzzled, Melissa looks at her questioningly.

Temporarily incapable of speech, Stella softly moves across the room, and like a parched desert flower welcoming rain, drinks in that face of surpassing loveliness, that face that mirrors her own when her world too was young. Glory transfigures her face as she says, in a voice that's half a sob, half a laugh, "So you still don't think I need to give you a birthday present?"

Melissa, now even more confused, says, "Of *course* you don't! Why are you—"

"Even—a *mother?* Oh my darling! My child born twenty-three years ago today in the old St. Helena Sanitarium— and her name was . . . her name is . . *Melissa!*"

EDITOR'S NOTE

I invite you to search out other stories of equal power, stories that move you deeply and that illustrate the values upon which this nation was founded. Many of these stories will be old, but others may be new.

Send me copies of the ones that have meant the most to you and your family, including the author, publisher, and date of first publication if at all possible. With your help, we will be able to put together additional collections (centered on other topics) for home, church, and school.

You may reach me by writing to:

Joe L. Wheeler, PhD
P.O. Box 1246
Conifer, Colorado 80433

May the Lord bless and guide the ministry of these poems and stories in your home.